Create a Better World

PSE Publishing
Louisville, Kentucky

"By far and away, the most popular column we have in the News-Leader is "Positively Speaking" written by Bob Mueller. Unlike other . . . columnists whose purpose is to make people think, laugh or get mad, Mueller writes to make us feel good about ourselves. His columns uplift the human spirit inside each of us and speak to our heart and soul. Any reader who takes a few minutes to read Mueller's column finds his/her spirit and attitude has changed for the better. *Look Forward Hopefully* . . . contains columns that are among the best of his practical inspirations."

"Mueller is a calm, patient counselor reaching out and embracing you. His writing style makes it feel it was written just for you. No lecturing, just a warm and new perspective to address your worry."

"*Look Forward Hopefully* belongs on a must read list of any person who needs good, simple, inspiration for peace and fulfillment."

— The Reporters, Inc. News-Leader

People who care for their own lives make the very best care-*givers*. Problem is — most of us don't really know how to provide optimal care for ourselves! In <u>The Gentle Art of Caring</u> Bob Mueller offers us practical, effective ways to enhance the way we think about our daily lives — then change the way we live them! Poignant and humorous stories and the sharing of his personal struggles to live a joyous and meaningful life make this book both true to life and a pleasure to read. Short, succinct chapters enable the reader to fit this book into *any* busy schedule. It should be read over and over and shared with everyone you love (and those you'd *like* to be able to love)!

- Jane M. Thibault, PhD.
Clinical Gerontologist, Division of Geriatrics
University of Louisville School of Medicine

Create a Better World

by

Bob Mueller

10/17/14

To Austin + Kaitlin,

Thanks for creating

a better world!

Bob Mueller

PSE Publishing
Louisville, Kentucky

Published and Distributed in the United States by
PSE Publishing
3902 Keal Run Way
Louisville, KY 40241
1-502-640-7811

Printed in the U.S.A.

10 9 8 7 6 5 4 3 2

Library of Congress Control Number: 2006937772
ISBN: 978-0-9744207-7-6

Cover design by Bernie Mudd
NAT Communication Resources

To Kathy
Who chooses, to love me unconditionally.
As my wife and lover,
She has taught me that love is something that never runs out.
Our true friendship will keep me happy all the days of my life.
Her loving and devoted support inspires me to
Create a Better World

Also by
Bob Mueller

Look Forward Hopefully
The Gentle Art of Caring

ACKNOWLEDGMENTS

A book begins as a creative thought in the author's mind. The road from the idea to publication is a long and arduous one. We are a sum total of what we have learned from all who taught us, both great and small. I am grateful for the inspiration and wisdom of these men and women and for the trans-generational sources and roots of wisdom they left to me. My road contained many supportive people whom I wish to gratefully acknowledge.

To Kathy Mueller, for her willingness to interrupt her schedule in response to my frequent requests to "just take a minute to read this bit and tell me what you think," I'm most thankful. I'm sure there is a special place in heaven for the spouses of authors. I thank her for shepherding this book from its earliest state to its present form. She has played the role of editor, critic, encourager and mentor.

For her insightful proofreading of this manuscript, I thank Stephanie Smith, a fellow Hospice colleague. I would also like to acknowledge Cathy Zion and Anita Oldham, publisher and editor for *Today's Woman* magazine, for publishing my columns for over fifteen years.

For those persons whose lives and writings have taught me to live with a little more dignity and a greater sense of wonder and awe: Charles Allen, Arthur Ashe, Dr. Wayne Dyer, Dorothy Day, Anthony de Mello, Joe Gallagher, Herman Hesse, Thomas Merton, Mother Teresa, Peace Pilgrim and John Powell.

To my family and my closest circle of friends who have called me to go deeper within myself and further out into the world, I offer my gratitude.

CONTENTS

Bob Mueller creates a better world, wherever he is. He sees, hears, and voices wisdom in life's everyday moments. He tunes into what matters most, while tuning out attitudes that can hinder or defeat.

Bob guides readers into their own worlds of insight, and calls us all to reach beyond ourselves. With tender grace and tenacious hope, he challenges us to be our best within ourselves and with others in our personal spheres of living, and throughout our global world.

Bob Mueller writes from what he lives; Bob lives what he writes. I've been privileged to know Bob as office neighbor and close colleague for some five-plus years. Day-to-day and season-through-season, Bob lives and breathes the essence of this book with honesty, authenticity, warmth, and humor. Bob Mueller creates a better world. Whether writing or speaking or just being "Bob," he inspires us all toward doing the same.

-Dr. Joy Berger, director, Hospice Institute;
author, *Music of the Soul: Composing Life Out of Loss.*

FOREWORD

Isn't that what each one of us wants ... to create a better world? I know I'd be thrilled if my epitaph read that "She created a better world."

Certainly, Bob Mueller's life and teachings have enabled many to improve their lot in life. As an inspirational and motivational writer, Bob has provided comfort and hope for the readers of Today's Woman magazine during the 11+ years he's written his monthly column. I know he's one of the main reasons the magazine is so loved by its readers.

And so when he asked to reprint some of his columns in compiling this book, I was quick to reply "Yes!" Bob will lighten your heavy heart, put a smile on your gloomy face, and sometimes hit a nerve that opens your eyes.

He's a philosopher, psychologist, clergyman, and scholar rolled into a really nice guy. I always feel better after reading Bob's words. And most of the time, I feel a little smarter as well. I'm sure you'll agree after reading "Create a Better World."

Cathy S. Zion
Owner & Publisher
Today's Woman magazine

INTRODUCTION

I feel as if, for the most part, I have lived affirmatively. That is, I have tried to concentrate on possibilities instead of problems. I believe it is better to emphasize our triumphs than our troubles. There is more power in accentuating our faith instead of our fears. There is more strength in thinking about the divine than about our sins. That's why I've entitled this book, *Create a Better World*.

Several years ago I picked up a hitchhiker. We came to a place where a new expressway was being built and there was a long detour over a rocky, dusty road. I began complaining about what it was doing to my car. I expressed disgust and frustration. After a while the hitchhiker said, "Mister, don't sweat the small stuff!" After that revealing comment, I quieted down, relaxed, and enjoyed the trip. I found myself repeating: "Don't sweat the small stuff." When we consider how short the journey of life really is, we must live affirmatively. I love the Swedish proverb:

> "Fear less, hope more; Eat less, chew more;
> Whine less, breathe more; Talk less, say more;
> Hate less, love more;
> and all good things will be yours."

One of the problems that I have had across the years is with people who emphasize the negative. Life is determined more by what we do than what we do not do. We come to moments of sorrow, of disappointment, of hurt. We have periods of depression and defeat. But during these times, if deep in our minds are some of the great positive truths contained in this book, they will give us the strength and stability to keep us going.

Once I was driving along the highway and the traffic was stopped. On the side of the road I saw some men placing large steel beams into the ground. I asked one of the men what he was doing. He explained to me that the ground under the road was shifting. They were sinking some of these beams to give stability to the roadbed.

I have always felt that it was of great value to sink great truths into one's mind. *Create a Better World*, like my first two books, *Look Forward Hopefully* and *The Gentle Art of Caring*, is my attempt to affect lives by sinking into life's greatest truths.

One of the best courses I ever took was a poetry class taught by priest and poet, Joe Gallagher, at St. Mary's Seminary & University in Baltimore, Maryland. It gave me a true appreciation for words.

Words are the raw material of every poem. According to poet W. H. Auden, a pre-requisite for any poet is a "passionate love of words." Such love will also intensify a reader's enjoyment of poetry, and exposure to good poetry will sharpen a reader's appreciation for words.

A poem is a verbal stained glass window. Its purpose is not only to let in light (meaning), but to do so through units of glass (words) which have various hues and shapes. These hues and shapes when combined in a particular way produce a special effect. If you showed someone a beautiful stained glass widow in your church, you wouldn't expect them to say, "My! It certainly does let the light in." The point is **the way** it lets the light in.

Too often we don't look **at** words or listen **to** them. Rather, we look or listen **through** them. Like a person looking through a window to see who is walking up the pathway, our mind's eye tends to focus exclusively on the **meaning** of words, so that we are scarcely conscious of the **medium** through which we attain messages.

In addition to their sound and shape, words have their own biography as part of their richness. I invite you to be nosey about their family background. Having studied Latin, Greek and Hebrew, I'm intrigued with the root origin of words. A few examples: **maudlin** (a weeping Mary **Magdalene** as painted by some artists); **tawdry** (cheap trinkets sold at **St. Audrey's** fair); **courtesy** (behavior at **court**); **saunter** (the pace of pilgrims to the Holy Land (Sainte Terre); **daisy** (day's eye: the sun with its rays); the kinship between the words: whole, heal, healthy, hale (and hearty) and hail! (be whole).

Some other interesting points about words include:

1. There are more than half a million words in the English language.
2. Twenty-five percent **of** all written **and** spoken English **is** made up **of** these ten words: the, of, and, I to, a, in, that, is, and it.
3. Fifty percent of all written and spoken English is made up of 50 basic words.
4. R. L. Thorndike, of dictionary fame, found that among the 1,000 English words used most often, only 36 have more than two syllables.
5. To quote Mark Twain, "The difference between the right and the nearly right word is the difference between lightning and a lightning bug."
6. Poet A. E. Houseman said he didn't so much bother about getting the right word as getting rid of the wrong one. Recall the sculptor who said he carved elephants by getting a piece of marble and chipping away whatever didn't look like an elephant.

I love the following letter from a man named Robert Pirosh applying for a job requiring verbal skills.

"Gentlemen, I like fat, buttery words such as ooze, turpitude, glutinous, and toady. I like solemn, angular, creaky words such as strait-laced, cantankerous, penurious, and valedictory. I like spurious, gold-plated, black-and-white words such as gentlefolk, mortician, free-lancer, or mistress. I like suave "V" words such as Svengali, svelte, bravura, and verve. I like crunchy, brittle, crackly words such as splinter, grapple, jostle, and crusty. I like sullen, crabbed, scowling words such as skulk, glower, scabby, and churl. I like Oh-heavens, my-gracious, land's-sake words such as tricky, tucker, genteel, and horrid. I like pretty-pretty, flowered endimanche words such as elegant, halcyon, Elysium and artiste. I like wormy, squirmy, mealy words such as crawl, blubber, squeal, and drip. I like sniggly, chuckling words such as cowlick, gurgle, bubble, and burp. I like words. May I have a few with you?"

Hopefully the words that follow will help you create a better world. Use these words to open your day and to calm your night.

PART ONE – Positive Words

Create a Better World

There are certain laws of life that, when followed, can make life sweeter, more harmonious, prosperous, healthy, and free. When we choose to abide by these laws, we reap the benefits of living in harmony with the universe. When we don't, we risk experiencing sickness, war, economic insecurity, and unemployment. A good way to create a better world is for each of us to be better people.

The problems that create turmoil, pain, misery, and suffering in our world can change when each person makes a conscious decision to act and think for the good of all. Personal motive is always a good guide. Ask yourself, "Why am I doing this?" and allow the inherent wisdom of spirit to provide the true answer. If your motives are pure, then good should come of them. The positive ideas we believe in today can constantly expand and grow in our consciousness.

Every human being also has a conscience. While we are in tune with the way things were designed to be, we are safe. When we are out of tune, we may show it in the form of greed, fear, sickness, addiction, and jealousy. Some people experience a lifetime of having the flu each winter, allergies in the fall, headaches, indigestion, and all the so-called minor ailments that they accept as a part of life. Sometimes it isn't necessary to suffer. With the help of physicians and science we can bring our physical body back in tune and enjoy life and its seasons.

An old farmer told me he was trying to get a stubborn old mule to move, but without success. He said someone told him, "Why don't you try your will power on that mule?" He replied, "I done tried it but it don't do no good. He's using his won't power."

Within each of us there are both will power and won't power. We may express lofty goals but at the same time tell ourselves that it's no use trying. We say, "I will" but our minds shout back at us, "You can't (you won't)."

"Won't power" is simply will power in reverse. It is easier for most of us to drift backward than to push forward. By always thinking and acting always with good in our hearts; by becoming responsible for ourselves; and by practicing the old Irish saying, "If you see a job that needs doing, that means it's yours to do," we can begin to change our wrong world into a right world, a better world.

It's time to stop saying that "they" need to be changing things around here. When we start saying, "I need to be giving life a helping hand," our lives benefit. It has been said that "a journey of a thousand miles begins with the first step." Let each one of us take that step and make it count.

The world needs good energy today as it has in the past. You and I are the ones who must provide it. If we, the people who say we value a meaningful life, don't do it, then who will? Certainly we must create a better world for it is in the space of spirituality and compassion where we will find the real life that we seek.

What You Offer the World

Years ago I had a life changing encounter at a Crisis Center in Baltimore with a young adult (let's call him "Hank") who had a history of drug abuse. He was about to commit suicide.

Hank had often visited the Crisis Center looking for meal passes and a night's lodging. If I noticed anything when I met Hank, it was that this boy wanted a twenty-four hour friend. He simply needed somebody to care about him.

One evening he came into the Crisis Center and as he sat down I noticed a pool of blood quickly forming under the chair. I jumped up and grabbed his arm. It was slashed, from the wrist to the elbow. This was prior to 911, so I called the operator and asked her to send the police immediately. Hank became hysterical. "Let me go, let me die!" There was blood everywhere.

As we raced to the hospital, my hands holding his wrists together, the police officer looked around into the back seat. The young policeman must have been a rookie. He advised, "You shouldn't play with razor blades kid, you could get hurt." I didn't say a word. What was there to say?

The following evening I visited Hank in the hospital. After a few quiet moments, he leaned over to me, handing me a knife, handle first and saying, "Here's my knife. I'll give you a chance to talk. Tell me why I shouldn't kill myself."

Before I could say a word, he started crying tears of frustration. "I haven't done anything important or made anything or won anything. No one listens when I talk, no one asks my opinion. I'm just there like a window or a chair. I seem to flop at everything. I don't try anymore because I'm afraid to fail. No one likes to fail all the time. If only there was something I could do, something I could rave about, something I could make that was my own. And people would say, 'Hank did that!' And my folks would smile and say,

'We're proud of you, son.' But I can't do anything. Everybody else is so much better at everything. The more I fail, the more it eats away at me until I feel weak all over. I feel like I'm nothing."

Hank asked me why he should go on living. I knew it wasn't for me to give him the answer. I could only listen and be a consoling friend, which was all he really needed. I could only assure him that eventually he would find his reason for existing if he kept searching.

That was many years ago. I've thought of Hank often and wondered what he found for his life. I couldn't answer then but now I'd like to attempt an answer by saying: the reason you should go on living, Hank (and all of us), is that the only hope the world has is **you**. The only hope it has is your having suffered and learned and, rather than become embittered, you became more whole, and learned what love is all about. Only then will you change and transform the corner of the universe where you find yourself. That's why we should exist. Because the world – those people walking the streets and loitering in bus stations going nowhere in a hurry – the world cries to you. And in elevating the world, you will discover that you will not only know the reason why you should live, but you will meet life itself.

We Are "Somebodies"

Have you ever felt left out or less than other people around you, whether it was at home, in school or on the job, like a nobody, even if only for a moment? In a sense, all of us have some feeling of inferiority. But there are three legitimate ways that we can deal with it.

First, recognize that you are needed in the world. Recently I was driving on a road in a rural community. I came to a place where the roads forked, but there was no sign indicating where each side went. I spotted a small store nearby and went over there to ask for directions to my destination. There were four men in the store, and all four started telling me how to get there at the same time. They each felt a sense of superiority in being called upon for help. That is always a stimulating experience. Every mother, social worker, physician, and every other person who serves people feels an immediate sense of worth.

There is a need in this world for every person to fill. I have a very close friend who has been extremely successful in life. He told me the turning point came when he was in high school. He was not making the highest grades in his class, and he was feeling defeated. Then a wise teacher said to him: "Stop trying to be the best and start being your best."

Maybe I cannot do as much as someone else, but at least I can do what I can do. Recognizing that there is a place of service for me is a very good place to start.

Second, we become important when we realize our possibilities. I picture in my mind a little baby and a puppy playing together on the floor. The puppy can run and jump. It can go over and drink water by itself and eat off a plate unassisted. In many ways, the puppy seems the superior creature. But you look at the two, and you realize that the puppy is going to grow up to be a dog. The baby is going to grow up to be a person. The possibilities of that little puppy are very limited, but the possibilities of that baby are almost endless. Recognizing that distinction makes a tremendous difference in the value we place on each one of them.

The same is true of us. Any one of us can say that we might not be all that we want to be now, but we have the possibilities of becoming far more than we are currently.

I read about a charm school, whose method included having the students stand before a full-length mirror and repeat their names in a soft, gentle voice "so as to impress oneself with oneself."

That method of teaching produces characters similar to a girl I read about once. Her name was Edith and the author described her as, "a little country bounded on the north, and on the south, and on the east, and on the west by Edith."

Standing for something greater than us is a third way of recognizing our possibilities and being our best selves. For example, think of two rooms: one room is lined on all four walls with mirrors; the second is wall to wall windows. In the first room we would only see ourselves; in the second room we would see the great world, which is all around us. It is vitally important in which room we choose to live our lives.

There is a purpose for every person. As we give our lives as best we can to the opportunities which we have been presented we are certain to accomplish and fulfill our purpose. That is success in life. We are "somebodies."

Create a Better World

Totally Awesome and
Simply Marvelous

Many young people today use the expression "totally awesome" to describe something or someone they find impressive. We might think the phrase is overused but instead it reminds me to spend time each day in awe, in total complete awe over the great things that surround me.

Dr. Wayne Dyer in his book <u>Real Magic</u> writes "a few minutes each day in total awe will contribute to your spiritual awakening faster than any metaphysics course." It's important to be thankful for your hands, your incomprehensively awesome mind, your best friends, your pet – the list goes on and on. It's enriching to treat all life with reverence and awe.

Every morning I ask myself five questions to create a positive state of mind and to keep me in awe about my life. They are:

1. What will I learn today?
2. Who will I reach out to today?
3. Who will I appreciate today?
4. How will I care for myself today?
5. Where will I see the positive today?

I often think of the story about the millionaire who owned a mansion on a hill overlooking the ocean. The owner told his close friend that he was going on a long trip and might be gone for some time. He asked this friend to move in and enjoy his mansion until he returned which could be sometime soon or never. The friend could wish that the millionaire never return or he could enjoy the mansion for whatever time he was there. He had a choice. In the life you and I have here on this earth, we need to always be grateful for what we have to enjoy now, in the moment and not be wishing away the future.

A phrase coined by Billy Crystal for the show *Saturday Night Live* that many people use is "simply marvelous" when they think something is wonderful. The refreshment that comes to a person filled with wonder is closely related to personal growth. Thomas Aquinas pointed out centuries ago that "no man can live without delight, and that is why a man deprived of joy of the spirit goes over to carnal pleasures." Many of our problems (persistent discouragement, depression, loneliness, feelings of inferiority, or obsession) can be traced to a common cause; we are starving our personalities. By depriving ourselves of the richness of wonder and delight we force ourselves to go scavenging for less wholesome mindsets.

I continue to marvel at all of creation. When you see big things – like the sky, mountains, and oceans; like friendship, love, and harmony – you think big thoughts. And when you think big thoughts, your life begins to grow and you rise above a multitude of little things that might harm you.

We have three small dogs in our home. Their entire world is our backyard and house. They hardly notice the sky except for an occasional chasing of birds. The only time they ever look up into a tree is if they are trying to catch a squirrel that has climbed out of their reach. They know us and love to be with us. They are content. So much of creation is wasted as far as our little dogs are concerned. There are also people who stay content in a very small world. They never consider the heavens or the unknown. They never really see anything big.

So, my challenge to you; take a look at something big – like the Alps in Europe. Think about how they were formed and how they've changed over thousands of years. There have been a multitude of thunderstorms, earthquakes and fires. They have known cold winters and the heavy burden of snow and ice. During their existence the wars of the world have come and gone; economic depressions, kings have come to power and fallen, civilizations have lived and died; but the Alps are still there. When seeing them or any

Create a Better World

mountain I feel stronger and more secure because of their immensity and their presence. All I can think is "totally awesome and simply marvelous."

Take a Different View

A man was planning a visit to New York and asked a friend who knew the city well to tell him what New York was really like. The friend told him that New York was both the best city in America and the worst. This friend said it would depend on what the visitor looked for. In New York he could find some of the most beautiful churches in the world. He could see some of the most famous paintings in the art galleries. He could hear some of the world's most glorious music. He could attend some of the finest dramatic productions in the world. He could dine in some of the nicest restaurants. Indeed, if he looked for it, he could find in New York the good, the beautiful and the true.

On the other hand, in that same city, he could find some of the most horrific slums. He could pass hardened criminals on the street. He could visit some of the cheapest and the most vulgar honky-tonks. There, he could associate with people who had sunk to the lowest level of life in every respect. If he wanted to look for it, he could find New York to be the very worst city. So, whether his visit to New York was to be one of joy and inspiration, or one of despair and discouragement, depended on what he looked for.

The same can be said of our lives and how we live. Up and down our own streets, we might see people with neighborly spirits and loving hearts. Or we might see pettiness and hatred in the lives of our neighbors. Our attitudes toward others are determined not by what people are, but by what we see in them. We can see the good, the true, in every person, or we can look for their faults and shortcomings.

If we are to experience lives of health, happiness and abundance, we must concentrate on love, light, beauty, truth and peace. If we let our minds shift to hatred, jealousy, lust, anger, failure, prejudice, or self-conceit, then our lives will be empty of light and filled with darkness.

Create a Better World

In "The Family Reunion" author T. S. Eliot has Harry saying, "I feel quite happy, as if happiness did not consist in getting what one wanted or in getting rid of what can't be got rid of, but in a different vision." In other words, we find happiness not by changing our circumstances, but in taking a different view of life.

The great tragedy in the lives of so many people is that they have eyes, but do not really see. Helen Keller was blind from the time she was a baby, yet through her life she saw the true beauties and wonders of the world. Once she said,

> "I have walked with people whose eyes are full of light but who see nothing in sea or sky, nothing in city streets, and nothing in books. It was far better to sail forever in the night of blindness with sense, and feelings, and mind, than to be content with the mere act of seeing. The only lightless dark is the night of darkness in ignorance and insensibility."

If you close your eyes to all opportunities for service, gradually darkness pervades your very soul and the light of your life will be extinguished. On the other hand if you are looking for and seeing opportunities to serve others through a gift, a kind and encouraging word, or an expression of love and interest, through giving of self to others, light comes into your life. So my friends, step out of the darkness and take a different view.

Take a Little Honey

"Take a little honey." Those were Jacob's words to his sons when they were going down into Egypt to buy food. They took many gifts – balm, spices, myrrh, nuts and money. But wise old Jacob added, "Take a little honey" (Genesis 43:11).

Honey is sweet, and when we use the term to describe an individual we think of them as gentle and kind. Without those qualities a person may struggle to succeed in the business of living.

I know people who on the journey of their lives have ability, training, initiative, ambition, faith, and so many other good things. Yet they failed because they forgot kindness. If they had just been a little sweeter in spirit and disposition what a difference it would have made.

The Talmud says there are ten strong things. Iron is strong, but fire melts it. Fire is strong but water quenches it. Water is strong, but the clouds evaporate it. Clouds are strong, but wind drives them away. People are strong, but fears cast them down. Fear is strong, but sleep overcomes it. Sleep is strong, but death is stronger. But loving kindness survives death.

Few people in American industry are paid a salary of a million dollars a year. One of those people was Charles M. Schwab. It has been said that Andrew Carnegie did not pay Schwab a million dollars a year because he knew more about steel than anyone else knew. In fact, he had a hundred people under him who knew more about steel than he knew. Carnegie paid him a million dollars a year because he knew how to get along with other people. That ability brought Schwab more than just financial gain. It brought him deep satisfaction in life.

When Mr. Schwab was past 70 years old, someone brought a nuisance suit against him. He easily won the suit in court, but before leaving the stand, he asked the judge's

Create a Better World

permission to say a few words. His comment that day is one of the most remarkable statements on kindness that we have recorded anywhere:

> "I'd like to say, here in a court of law, and speaking as an old man, that nine-tenths of my troubles are traceable to my being kind to others. Look, you young people, if you want to steer away from trouble, be hard-boiled. Be quick with a good loud no to anyone and everyone. If you follow this rule, you'll be seldom molested as you tread life's pathway." "Except," and the great man paused, a grand smile lighting his kindly features, "except – you'll have no friends, you'll be lonely – and you won't have any fun!"

And I love John Boyle O'Reilly's poem on "What is real good?"

> "What is real good?
> I'm in musing mood.
>
> Order, said the law court;
> Knowledge, said the school;
> Truth, said the wise man;
> Pleasure, said the fool;
> Love, said a maiden;
> Beauty, said the page;
> Freedom, said the dreamer;
> Home, said the sage;
> Fame, said the soldier;
> Equity, the seer.
>
> Spake my heart full sadly,
> "The answer is not here."
> Then within my bosom

Softly this I heard:
"Each heart holds the secret;
Kindness is the word."

Kindness is described as being love in action. It is those things we do. In this connection, we think of the well-known words of William Penn. He said, "I expect to pass through life but once. If therefore, there be any kindness I can show, or any good thing I can do to any fellow-being, let me do it now, and not defer or neglect it, as I shall not pass this way again." Or as my wife always says to me when she knows by the frown on my face that I am about to say something negative or caustic, "Honey, be kind."

Push the Happy Button

A friend described a woman who always bubbled over with joy each morning when she arrived in the office where he worked each morning. Many of the other employees stared into a newspaper, out into space, or over a half-filled cup of coffee. But this woman touched each person with her joy and enthusiasm. One day when asked what her secret was, she replied, "I push the happy button before I get up each day." "The happy button?" someone asked. "What is that?"

"Well," she responded, "Before I get up, I remind myself that this is a fresh, new day. I count my blessings. Then I laugh for the sheer joy of being alive and get up and start my day! Push the happy button for yourself and see what happens."

My friend did push the happy button the next day. He remarked that he has been doing it ever since and found it a marvelous way to begin the morning, and especially if the day promised to be a busy one. He was also following the wisdom of the French writer Colette, who said, "Be happy. It's one way of being wise."

Years ago I met Mother Teresa of Calcutta when she spoke at a local university. A retired priest in a wheelchair wanted to hear her speak and I had the honor of accompanying him to the front row. After her talk she spent five minutes talking with the two of us. Mother Teresa epitomized better than anyone the concept that happiness can be achieved by what you do. She believed in showing love to those who are near and to those who cross our path every day. A powerful reward of loving service is the deep inner knowing that you have given the greatest gift – yourself – and that is happiness money can't buy.

A lot of people know in their hearts that there is great value in happiness. What do you really like to do? What brings you the greatest fulfillment? If these are the things that take up your time, then you are probably happy. If you can use more happiness in your life, try pushing the happy button and you may find a rewarding, useful, and spiritually satisfying experience.

We often make statements like these: "If only I had a new bike, then I'd be happy. If only my family were more understanding, then I'd be happy. If only my hair were styled better. If only I had more friends. If only . . ." Sometimes we begin to sound like a broken record when things go wrong, so certain that if the events and conditions of our lives were different, we'd be happy.

It's an old and unfortunate habit that we look around outside ourselves for happiness. We can never be sure of it if we count on certain conditions to guarantee it. However, we can always be sure of happiness if we carry it with us wherever we go. We can develop the happiness habit, with practice, just as surely as good piano playing or accurate pitching. We can control our own thoughts. The decision to make them happy ones is ours to make.

Create a Better World

Positive Thinking

There was a lady who rented a jeep to do some heavy work. Having been told that a jeep could go anywhere, she drove down on the beach and became mired in some soft sand. She raced the motor but instead of pulling out, the jeep just dug deeper into the sand. She gave up and walked to a nearby garage to get a wrecker to come and pull the jeep out.

The garage owner explained she didn't need the wrecker, but he went with her to show her what to do. He pointed to a gearshift lever that she had not noticed and explained that the jeep has a pulling gear. He showed her how to operate it, and the jeep drove right out of the sand. He thought, "That lady thought she was stuck, but she had more power than she realized. She just wasn't using it."

There are vast numbers of people who feel defeated in their lives. Their conqueror may be guilt for a wrong action, or it may be a mental block, such as fear or worry. I am convinced that no person need be defeated by themselves. You have within reach the power to live victoriously.

We frequently encounter difficulties which stop our progress and hold us back because we forget we have a "pulling gear." We get mired up in a sticky situation or uncomfortable circumstance. But within us is a marvelous power that can keep us going. Some people call that power "positive thinking." It is the positive action, represented by belief and faith that leads to the victory.

Remember the woman in the jeep. She might have spent hours digging away at the sand, but that would not have gotten her jeep out. Instead, she needed to turn on the power to pull through the sand. Reforming our lives is not enough. It is through faith and belief, through positive thinking and action that the failures and misdeeds of our lives are overcome and we pull ourselves out of the defeat that holds us back.

We never gain power over the weaknesses and wrongs of our life until we admit to them and face them honestly. We must be willing not only to let them go, but also to make whatever effort is required in ridding our life of those negative influences. Take action. Engage the pulling gear.

That is not easy because you must deal with your mind and the mind can be the biggest liar in the world. It will trick you if it can. First it will try to get you to believe that certain things are not wrong. "Other people do those same things, and they get along all right," our minds will tell us. Or the mind may tell you to wait until next year to change a bad habit. Or the mind may convince you that you are weak and you just can't change.

People who have vacation cottages know how much work is required each year to open the house for the summer. Even though every room was spotless when closed up the previous fall, they return to dust, bugs and cobwebs. One trouble with an empty house is it won't stay empty. You can clean it up, move everything out and lock the door but dust will gather.

So it is in the house of life. Left empty, uninvited and undesirable tenants move in. After positive action is taken, there must be continuous follow-up. In the First World War, the allied armies defeated the Kaiser but did nothing really constructive to strengthen European troops; then Hitler, moved in. If we fail to continue to replace our wrongs with positive works and influences, eventually the wrongs will come back with much stronger force.

Believe, create in your mind a picture of the person you want to be. Keep that picture before you, let it occupy your thinking, and there will be no place for thought of the negatives which will want to come back into your life.

Create a Better World

PART TWO – Lessons to Learn

Learn to Love Yourself

The more you study this world, the surer you become that everything is significant. For example, an apple falling from a tree may seem utterly unimportant – except that when Isaac Newton saw it, he discovered the law of gravity. It unlocked untold numbers of scientific doors for the good of society.

When I was growing up, every morning in many homes, a teakettle was placed on the stove and heated. For us, the boiling water simply meant a cup of tea or a cup of coffee. To Robert Fulton it became the principle of the steam engine. This invention literally made possible much of the industry which lead to the development of the Industrial Revolution. We need to remember that there is no insignificant moment or experience and – most importantly – "person."

While studying the history of the Adams family, a researcher came across the diary of Charles Francis Adams. He found that one day the only words recorded were, "WENT FISHING WITH SON. DAY WASTED." The son was named Brooks Adams, and in his writing, he referred to that day which he had spent fishing with his father. He described how the fish were not biting and how they did not catch even one. Instead, they sat talking. Brooks was twelve years old at the time, but he asked his father many questions, and his illustrious father explained to him many of the most important aspects of life. Later on, Brooks Adams, in recalling that day, said, "This was the most significant changing point in my life." For one, it was a "day wasted." For the other it was "life-changing."

There are really no insignificant events, no wasted days, and no unimportant people. Learning to love you is really the starting place.   Learning to love you is not narcissism. Excessive admiration of self or self involved fascination with you is not the kind of love for yourself that is appropriate. Some people never grow out of their infantile stage of development, in which the self is the object of one's love interest.   Learning to love yourself is not falling in love with your own image.   Narcissism literally blocks proper love for oneself and develops very deep seeded self-hatred.   In this state human relationship cannot be fully experienced.

Whether it is loving God, or loving other people, or loving yourself, it is important to remember that love is one package.   It cannot be divided.   The person who does not love himself or herself will not be a balanced or happy person.   The basic problem is that these individuals focus solely on themselves to compensate for the perceived lack of acceptance by others.   They block God out of their lives, and they unconsciously avoid human relationships.

The precept that our attitudes begin with ourselves is beautifully expressed in a poem entitled "A Life in Your Hands."

If a child lives with criticism,
    He learns to condemn.
If a child lives with hostility,
    He learns to fight.
If a child lives with ridicule,
    He learns to be shy.
If a child lives with shame,
    He learns to feel guilty.
If a child lives with tolerance,
    He learns to be patient,
If a child lives with encouragement,
    He learns confidence,
If a child lives with praise,
    He learns to appreciate,
If a child lives with fairness,

Create a Better World

He learns justice,
If a child lives with security,
He learns to have faith,
If a child lives with approval,
He learns to like himself,
If a child lives with acceptance and friendship,
He learns to find love in the world.
-Dorothy Law Holte

Loving yourself does not mean excluding others. Genuine self-love is never egocentric or selfish. True self-love is mirrored in our attitude toward God and others. We look at others through the attitudes that we have toward ourselves. Learning to love you is really the starting place.

Rid Your Spirit of Infirmity

Have you ever sat in an airport and watched people or listened to conversations around you in a crowded restaurant? It is sad to see so many people stumbling through life feeling defeated, unhappy, frustrated, and often bitter and disappointed. Life can be a wonderful experience every day.

When it feels like something is dragging us down, we can gain the upper hand and find new confidence by doing three things. First, be willing to understand and accept ourselves. The great psychologist William James quoted a woman as saying, "The happiest day in my life was the day I admitted the fact that I am not physically beautiful and stopped worrying about it."

A woman told me that all of her life she has been underweight. She said that people would talk about how thin she was and it concerned her. She explained that she worried about getting sick. Then one day her physician said to her, "You were born skinny and will be all your life, so stop trying to do anything about it." Through her doctor she now understands her body type and accepts herself as she is. She is still skinny but that fact is not on her mind; it is not a problem to her any longer.

In the play *Green Pastures*, Noah says, "I ain't much, but I'se all I got." When we accept that fact, life takes on new meaning and power. All of us have handicaps of one sort or another. We can let the handicap affect our minds and defeat us, or we can go on in spite of ourselves and be a winner in life.

General William Booth, founder of the Salvation Army and one of the great men of all time, was informed that he was going blind. He said, "I have done what I could for God with two eyes. Now I will do what I can without any eyes."

Create a Better World

There is a second step to gaining self assurance. Ask your Higher Power for help. I love the prayer I learned from a humble old man years ago: "Lord, help me to understand that You are going to let nothing happen that You and I can't handle together." If I thought I had to do the things I have planned for the next twelve months by myself, with only my own strength and resources, I would give up and quit this minute.

One of the reasons people lose confidence and get shaky is that they realize they do not have the abilities and strength to do the things they feel they must do. But I don't depend only on myself. I know there are other people who will help me.

I have proposed two things, understand and accept yourself and trust in the help of your Higher Power and other people. I have one more thing to offer, get started living your faith the best you can.

The president of a furniture company had a large number of people working for him. Had the opinion that no one person was indispensable; he could always get another to replace any one of his employees. Gradually he came to feel that there was one girl in his office who was the exception. He could not explain why that girl was so important. She had no special qualifications. Others did their work as well as she. But he felt the office simply could not go on without her.

Finally he asked her about herself, and she gave him a brief answer outlining her life and then said, "One day changed my life forever." She told of hearing a sermon in which the minister had said, "Why not dedicate yourself to others for just one day?" The minister explained that the average life spans about half a million hours. Surely one could afford to use at least 24 of those hours in such a noble experiment. The girl decided to try it.

That night she had a feeling of happiness and satisfaction she had not known before. So, naturally, she decided to try it a second day and she did. Each day she would promise, "I'll try dedicating myself to others for just this one day." When she was tempted to be her old self in some situation, she would remember the satisfaction she had felt since dedicating herself to others, and she would gain the inspiration to keep going. As the days went by, it became easier for her and life became a joyful experience. Over time that became her philosophy of life.

Later this same woman wrote as she continued to grow in her spirituality, "Imagine what it means never to be afraid of anything. Not to be afraid of insecurity, of loss of position, not to be afraid of life or death. Imagine what it means to have no ill will. Imagine what it is to be at peace. I suddenly discovered that everything began to flow toward me rather than away from me. Amazing things happened. Life became good and everybody seemed to love me. Gradually I began to have a sense of well-being."

The "one-day" idea worked wonders for her. Why don't you try it? And wouldn't this be a good day to begin the experiment?

Overcoming Feelings of Inferiority

How do you overcome feelings of inferiority? That is something nearly every person would like to know. Most of us have moments when we feel inadequate. We often feel inferior as we face the unknown and challenging circumstances of our lives.

A man I was visiting in the hospital recently said to me, "It's no use. This disease is bigger than me and I can't handle it." His doctor said he could make a complete recovery if he would only begin to believe in himself and his power to heal. But he has accepted defeat and surrendered to it. It is much easier to surrender to an inferiority complex than to overcome it, and a lot of people have done just that.

But to those who really want to gain confidence and personal power, to those who are unwilling to give up, there is a threefold path to follow:

- Consider your own strength and power,
- Face up to your giant, and
- Trust in God's help.

David was not the last person to be confronted by a giant. In fact, we all have our giants and that is why so many people develop inferiority complexes. If there were no giants, you would not feel inferior.

Some of the giants in our lives are real. Others are imaginary. But whether they are real or not, the trouble comes when we allow the giants to make us insignificant; when, instead of giving our best, we give up and quit. Your giant may be a physical handicap; it may be a difficult job; it may be a deep sorrow, a financial debt, a feeling of loneliness, or a harmful habit. David did not minimize the strength of the giant; neither did he let the giant minimize him. The first step to overcoming those feelings is to consider your own strengths and power, as well as the force of the adversary in your life.

The second step is to go forth and do battle with the giant. You will never win a fight if you don't fight. One reason many people have an inferiority complex is that they try to be someone else instead of themselves. The secret of success is to determine what you have and then have the courage and energy to use it.

The Saturday afternoon before I was to preach my first sermon as associate pastor at a new church, I was in the sanctuary alone. It seemed so big and strange to me that I was almost paralyzed by fear. Much younger then, I knew nothing about a big city church. I was afraid that I would fail miserably. Then I walked down the aisle and knelt at the altar and prayed. I felt a calm spirit coming over me, and I left the church that day with joy and peace in my heart.

When we stand at our full height in the face of obstacles, when we refuse to shrink back but instead give our own best, when we sincerely say to life, "I will give my very best everyday," the inhibitions are taken away, the tangles are cleared, and the clouds of life are lifted.

Down But Not Out

I met a lovely girl the other day and noticed she was wearing an engagement ring. I asked, "When do you plan to get married?" She barely whispered, "He died last year." That girl is on the roadside of life, wounded. A young couple talked about the recent death of their only child. They felt without him their journey through life has lost much of its meaning. They, too, are by the roadside, wounded.

A dear friend is in the hospital. Her health has been compromised by an accident that will leave her an invalid the rest of her life. She understands the facts of her case but she too has been left personally wounded. In so many ways we can be hurt and join the waiting wounded. Often, it seems, when we are making our greatest progress and when life is at its best, a "disaster" big or small becomes the thief that takes away what we loved so much and leaves us on the highway of life, wounded.

There was a story in the paper about a man who stayed at home one Fourth of July. He said it was too dangerous to be out on the highway. While he was sitting in his backyard, a bolt fell off of an airplane flying overhead and hit him, causing a severe injury. I know of a man who refused to fly in an airplane because he felt it was too dangerous. Yet one day he slipped in the bathtub and broke his neck. We might say the first man should not have been sitting out in the yard, but we hardly would want to say the other man should not have been taking a bath.

There are times when we are in no position to be a Good Samaritan. Instead, we find ourselves as the one wounded and left by the roadside. There are three realizations that might help.

1. **To be wounded means you still have life.** As long as there is life there is hope. Over the years we have been thrilled by the story of Ben Hogan. His car was hit by a large bus, and he lay wounded

by the roadside. It was doubtful he would ever walk again. A great career in golf was ended, we thought. As soon as possible he got leg braces and began to swing his golf clubs. It was painful, but he kept swinging and came back to win both the United States and the British championships. As long as there is life there is hope.

2. **When you are wounded, you can count on help coming your way.** Often it is help you did not expect. When philosopher and writer Jean Jacques Rousseau was hunted and hounded from one place to another because of his opinions, Voltaire heard of it and although Voltaire did not share Rousseau's views, he invited him to come and live in his home. And when Rousseau finally arrived, Voltaire embraced him and said, "I do not agree with a word you say, but I will fight to the death for your right to say it."

3. **Don't let your wounds make you bitter.** The story is told that Louis B. Mayer, the movie man, got into a fight once when he was a school boy and came out on the losing end. At home that night he muttered hateful words against the other boy and vowed to get even. His mother heard him but said nothing then. The next day the Mayer family went on a picnic out in the mountains. Louis' mother called him over to a little clearing that faced a mountain wall. She told him to say what he said last night. He was ashamed but she insisted and he said, "Damn you." She told him to shout it like he had the night before. He did, and from the mountains all around came his words back to him saying, "Damn you." Then his mother told him to shout, "Bless you." He did, and the whole world seemed to be saying back to him, "Bless you," as the echo of his voice came back.

Louis Mayer understood and the law of the echo became the law of his life. Life itself carries with it the possibility of being hurt. If a person had absolutely no feeling of any kind, he or she could not be hurt, but a person without feeling would be considered among the living dead. So the fact that you can be wounded is a sign that you are alive.

A Short Course on Human Relations

There are many books on how to win friends, the art of popularity, and human relations in general. By far the best thing ever written on such subjects is the twelfth chapter of Paul's Letter to the Romans centuries ago. Any person who learns and applies the principles listed there will never lack for friends. Putting just a few into practice will add a new dimension to friendships, family and work relationships.

1. *"Not to think of ourselves more highly than we ought to think."* The quickest pathway to unpopularity is conceit. However, that does not mean that we must wear the cloak of total humility. The true way to be humble is to stand tall and always do your best.

People sometimes say a nice word to me about my writing, and I appreciate it, but I would never get conceited over it, because I am an avid reader and have read many of the really great writers of our time. When I read one who is far superior to me and realize how far short I fall, it is hard not to be humble and do my best at the same time.

The same principle can be applied in your life. Do your very best, but remember there will always be others who are greater than you, and you will have no trouble keeping conceit in check.

2. *"We, who are many, are one body."* This is simply saying that there are millions of people, and that it takes us all to make the world. It means to recognize that every person's place is important.

What if a fountain pen remarked, "I am writing the book." Then the ink replied, "No, I am writing the book. You could not make a mark if it were not for me." "Well" the paper replied, "But what could either of you do without me?" Then the dictionary added, "If I did not supply the

Create a Better World

words no book could be written." And all during the argument the author just smiled.

3. *"Hate what is evil, hold fast to what is good."* The real basis of healthy relationships is respect, and no person has either their own self-respect or the respect of others who refuses to stand for good and against evil. Good is drawn to good and evil seeks out evil. You choose your relationships.

4. *"Be patient in suffering."* Constant complaining and sympathy seeking never wins friends. Every person has his sorrows, and it does not make anyone like you better for you to try to suggest that yours are the worst anyone has ever had.

There was an old man who was always thankful. Then he was struck down by a severe sickness with chills and fevers. A friend said, "I don't think you have anything to be thankful for now?" He replied, "Oh, yes, when I have the fever I am thankful for chills that cool me off, then I am thankful for the fever that warms me up again."

No matter how bad your trouble is, there is always some reason for gratitude.

5. *"Bless those who persecute you; bless and do not curse them . . . overcome evil with good."* When we are facing the question, "What should I do?' one way that helps to decide is to ask, "What would happen if I did the opposite?" Apply that here. Instead of loving your enemy, decide that you are going to hate your enemy. Do you feel, even for one moment, this is the better course? Was Abraham Lincoln wrong when he said, "With malice toward none; with charity for all"? Did Booker T. Washington make a mistake when he said, "I am resolved that I will permit no man to narrow and degrade my soul by making me hate him"? Surely no one of us feels that Booker T. Washington would have been a better man had he returned hate for the insults he received for the color of his skin.

There are at least ten other principles as important as these five I have mentioned in this chapter of St. Paul. Read the twelfth chapter of Romans carefully every morning and every night for one month and you will see a distinct difference in your attitude toward other people and in their attitude toward you.

The "If Only I Had" Game

I was riding with a dear friend of mine in an area of my home town. He pointed out some land to me and said that he considered buying the property some 20 years ago. He had even gone so far as to arrange the financing with his bank, but decided against the purchase. He told me, "The property is now worth 30 times more than it would have cost back then." He talked about how much money he would have today, if he had gone ahead and completed the transaction. Then with a smile, he turned to me and said, "However, long ago, I learned you can't play that 'If only I had' game." All of us can look back and say, "If only I had done this, or if only I had . . ."

We think of our children and wish we had done some things differently. The same can be said about marriage, or of jobs, or most all of our life experiences.

I am reminded of a lady about 40 years old who is having extreme mental and emotional problems. Her mother died two years ago, and ever since she has been worrying about some things she said to her mother long ago and she is plagued by regret. We can all look back on experiences with regrets. Regrets aren't bad in themselves, but those regrets can turn into abnormal guilt. There is normal guilt and there is abnormal guilt. Normal guilt is something we face, do what we can about it, and go on. Abnormal guilt takes possession of us and has the power to literally destroy us often echoing with the phrase, "If only I had. . ."

It is probably true that as most people move toward the latter part of life, the one thing they would rather have than anything else is the forgiveness for the mistakes they have made and the sins they have committed.

We can be thankful that most people are merciful. Normally, parents do not remember every unkind thing their children said or did. Most friends don't hold grudges forever. Most of our sins and mistakes have already been forgiven.

The hardest forgiveness to acquire is our own. Guilt that is not diffused can cause misery for a lifetime. Let's remember that we all are guilty and there comes a time when guilt needs to stop. If something can be done, do it. If nothing can be done, dismiss it and go on. You will never forget, but you can forgive yourself.

A young woman I know was in a serious automobile accident. She was thrown into the windshield, and the glass cut her face severely. When I first saw her in the hospital, she was so thankful and grateful that her life had been spared. The wreck was very serious and it was a miracle that she had not been killed. She expressed gratitude to God for her life and felt that because God had spared her, she wanted to live for others as she had never done before. She talked about volunteering at a home for children in need.

But later as she recovered from her physical injuries, she took a closer look at the scars on her face. The surgeons had done a good job in minimizing the scars, but still they were there and she felt ugly. The facial disfigurement was not nearly as severe as the damage in her mind. This is true many times of our own problems. They have a way of growing out of proportion, if we continue to dwell on them. Gradually, the young woman spoke less and less of her gratitude to God for being saved, and more and more of the resentment she had for the scars on her face.

Resentment is an emotion that most of us have felt, and it's almost always destructive. It's to be expected, not to be nursed and cultivated and allowed to grow. I know men who, never got a break in life. They look at others who have prospered and realize that they have as much ability, and gradually began to feel that life's not fair. "My house should be as good as my neighbor's; my position in the community should be respected; I should have more money." Resentment can become poison. Hostilities can grow to the point that we believe that life is unfair, and that God does not love us. However, it helps us to remember that this is also a

Create a Better World

normal reaction to life's disappointing experiences. We need to assure ourselves that resentments can be overcome and we can start by not saying, "If only I had . . ."

Don't Be Afraid To Ask

When I was six years old my family lived in a small town in the Midwest. One Saturday, a store was handing out baseball caps to children. Any boy or girl who wanted a hat could go into the store, ask for it, and get it. I watched other youngsters go in and come out proudly, each wearing one of those caps. Finally, I got up enough nerve to go in. When I saw there was only one cap left, I lost my nerve, and without saying a word, turned, and walked out. One of my friends asked me, "Did you get a cap?" I told him, "No." But I didn't tell him that I didn't ask for one.

When I recall this childhood incident it makes me think that most of the time people lose out on the things they want by simply not asking for them.

All of us have causes and values we passionately believe in. If you strongly believe in something, you are willing to ask for support from others for your cause. When you do not believe deeply, you may begin to be negative. You might hear yourself say, "I cannot do that," or, "That is too good for me to hope for," or, "There is no reason for me to try." There is no way of measuring what we miss because we never learn to believe, and, not believing, we never ask.

There are four basic principles for asking:

1. **Decide what you really want.** You have a marvelous ability called *imagination*. Actually, it is like having a motion-picture screen in your mind. You can put a picture on that screen and look at it. When you are thinking of your life, keep putting the picture of what you really want on the screen of your mind. Put it on, change it, and shift it. Keep working at it, until that picture is clearly focused.

   Then test that picture with such questions as: *Is it good for me? Is it fair to all concerned? Am*

I ready for it now? When that mental picture measures up to our highest tests, then you are ready. Do not hesitate.

2. **Ask.** Many years ago I heard a story that impressed me deeply, and many times I have used this same technique of asking. The story was about a man who, every night when he went to bed, would put his keys in his shoe. The next morning, when he started to put on his shoe, his foot would touch those keys. He would take the keys out and say to himself, "There are doors that are locked, but locked doors will not stop me, because these keys will unlock those doors." Then he would ask for strength and pray, *Lord, when I come up against some situation today — one that seems to be blocking my path — instead of feeling defeated, let me realize there is a key to every situation, and help me look for and find that key.*

3. After you see the picture and after you ask, the third step is to **commit to do what you can do.** I know a lady who is an outstanding corporate executive. She tells how she got her first job as a stenographer. She wanted to be more than a stenographer, but she realized that she did not have the qualifications. She enrolled in night school, and began to study accounting and business procedures and other courses that would help her in her work. Working all day and then going to school at night was not easy. But she kept on, and she applied that knowledge to qualify herself for higher positions. At each step she recommitted herself to take additional coursework to prepare for the next potential promotion.

4. **Let us ask, believing.** Believing includes dreaming, feeling, and acting, and not in any particular order. Some people begin by dreaming, and then begin seeking to make that dream a reality. Others start with doing what they can do, and then develop dreams as they go. The important thing is to begin and move forward. Feelings too can bring about dreams. It really does not matter where we begin; what matters is that we start.

I find help sometimes in the first four letters of the alphabet to inspire me to ask for what I desire:

A stands for ask.

B stands for believing.

C stands for commitment.

D means doing something about it

Ask, believe, commit, and then, do something.

Learning to Forgive

I recently talked with a man who was in such a nervous state he could not do his work. His business was going down, his home life was unhappy, he was avoiding his friends, and had started drinking heavily.

We found that his trouble stemmed from a terrible thing he had done some years before. He had tried to forget it, but the thought of it was increasingly in his mind. He would think about it during the day and even dreamed about it at night. His mind had become almost completely obsessed by this one memory.

It was something that required no restitution, and now there was nothing he could do about it. But he was deeply repentant and seemed to me to meet every condition of forgiveness. I read and explained to him the Fifty-first Psalm, which is David's prayer of repentance.

I feel absolutely sure that God completely forgave that man that day. I told him that and he believed it and I believed he would be all right.

But the next week he came back, no better than he had been. I said to him, "God has done something for you that you are unwilling to do for yourself. You asked God to forgive you and God did, but you have not forgiven yourself." He agreed, but insisted he could not get it out of his mind.

There are many people who are living a condemned life because they never learned to accept the forgiveness of God, and therefore, to forgive themselves. Many people carry an accumulation of past mistakes, failures, and sins. It becomes a burden that no person can bear. It produces terrific mental strain, nervousness, fear and worry. Walt Whitman said: "I think I could turn and live with animals, they are so placid and self-contained . . . They do not lie awake in the dark and weep for their sins."

One can be so overwhelmed with a sense of guilt that one of three things happens. We could be turned into a being without conscience or hope. Or life might become unbearable. Or we can accept forgiveness and be free – God's forgiveness, and then our own.

Time and again I have read to myself and to others a poem that Ernest Rogers wrote long ago, which he called "Another Chance." One of the verses goes:

> But down on my trembling knees I fall,
> Though others may look askance,
> To say a prayer to the Lord of All.
> The God of another chance.

A minister tells of a lady in his church who was on a ministry committee. It was announced that a meeting of the committee was to be held at the home of another committee member. The lady said to the minister, "After what she did, I will not set foot in her house."

The minister asked her when she joined that church. She told him 27 years ago. Then he began to name each one of the ministers who had been at that church during those years. He pointed out that each one was a capable and faithful preacher of the gospel. Then he said, "You mean to say that for 27 years in this church, you have sat here as the love of Christ was preached and now you say you will not 'set foot in this woman's house'"? Then sadly he added, "What have you heard in church?"

It is so easy to keep account of wrongs against us, to be too sensitive, to look for evil when none was intended. But love through forgiveness refuses to be insulted or to be hurt. There is toughness and strength in love that protects one's heart and feelings, like a suit of armor protects the body.

The Duke of Wellington was about to pronounce the death sentence on a convicted deserter. Deeply moved, the great General said, "I am extremely sorry to pass this severe sentence, but we have tried everything, and all the discipline and penalties have failed to improve this man who is otherwise a brave and good soldier."

Then he gave the man's comrades an opportunity to speak for him. "Please, you're Excellency," said one of the men, "There is one thing you have never tried. You have not tried forgiving him." The General forgave him and it worked; the soldier never again deserted and ever after showed his gratitude to the Iron Duke.

The primary reason most of us do not forgive is simply because we do not want to. Before you realize it, bitterness against another person will spread through your system like a fast growing cancer. It will make you angry and irritable. You may develop a martyr-complex, and you begin to pity yourself. Before long you begin to enjoy your misery. Gradually you become a helpless creature. To cure a body afflicted with cancer is far easier than to take an unforgiving spirit out of one's soul. For forgiveness is our deepest need and highest achievement.

Music Lessons

One of the greatest gifts my mother gave me was music lessons. I was blessed to have a terrific teacher named Sister Vincentia who taught me to play the piano during my junior high years. Sister was strict, intelligent, witty, and highly motivated to get the most from each of her students. Some of my greatest insights about life came from her music lessons.

Sister would make all of her pupils practice the conclusions of their recital pieces over and over again. Invariably we would grumble because of the constant repetition of the last few measures of music. When we voiced our complaints, she would always answer, "You can make a mistake in the beginning or you can make a mistake in the middle. The people will forget it if you make the ending glorious."

Even though Sister Vincentia was very strict, she always told us how special we were as musicians. One of her favorite stories was about a great violinist who thrilled the audience with his playing. At the end of the selection, he smashed his violin into a hundred pieces over a chair. The people sat aghast. Then he picked up another violin and said, "Don't be alarmed. The one I smashed was purchased for only a few dollars in a shop down the street. I shall now play my Stradivarius." He played the same selection but the majority of the people could not tell the difference. Then the violinist said, "Friends, so much has been said about the value of my violin that I wanted to impress upon you the fact that the music is not in the instrument; it is in the one who plays upon it."

Sometimes as young musicians, we would worry about what might go wrong at a recital. What if I mess up? What if a key on the piano is broken? Sister would say, "What if? What if?" Then she would launch into another violinist story. She told of a great violinist who was giving a concert when the "A" string on his violin broke. Without hesitating, he transposed the music and finished the concert on three strings. A lesser violinist might have stopped and moaned about his bad luck. It takes a great artist to say, "If I can't play on four strings, I'll play on three." She would point out that we can complain about our bad fortune, or we can go ahead and produce melody with what we have.

One time I asked Sister Vincentia, "Where does music come from?" She told me that nobody really knows. A painter paints some object; a poem is an expression of intelligence, but music is a mystery. Out of the "everywhere" comes melody. Music was not invented; it was pressed upon our souls.

Oliver Wendell Holmes once said, "Many people die with their music still in them." Sister's music lessons always taught us to develop and to be true to ourselves. She loved to tell the story of the authenticity of the composer Mozart. When Mozart was 25 years old, he went to Vienna. One day his publisher said to him, harshly, "Write, sir, in a more easy and popular style; or I will neither print your music nor pay you a penny for it."

Mozart and his wife were so poor that they often had neither food nor fuel in their tiny house. One cold morning that winter, a friend who came to visit Mozart found his house entirely without heat and the composer and his wife waltzing to keep warm. In fact, the cold and hunger put him in his grave when he was 35.

It must have been an almost unbearable temptation to him to sacrifice his standards. He might so easily have said, "After all, a man has to eat." Or he may have more easily said, "I cannot see my wife suffer." Instead, he said to his publisher, "Then, my good sir, I have only to resign and die of starvation. I cannot write as you demand."

Sister Vincentia would add to the story, "And starve he did; but isn't the world proud of him? The faith he kept is still keeping him." This music teacher taught me at an early age that there is something within every person which, if given a chance, will make that person invincible. That something is the spark of divinity within.

The Passing of Time

To an adult an oak tree is just a tree, a cloud passing before the moon is just a cloud like those that have gone before. But to a child that same tree is a jungle gym and that same cloud is an elephant in the sky. Things happen for the first time to a child. The world is born fresh with each moment of time.

I remember an August day when my brother was four and I 15. After supper my dad, brother and I went for a walk. We approached an open field with a row of oaks behind it. My brother had been grasping my hand, but now he slipped free. He stood quietly for a moment, this big-city boy, surveying the largest expanse of earth he had ever seen that was entirely void of people. And then he was off, running hard, the wind blowing his hair and the sun shining on his full round cheeks.

I can still close my eyes and envision him, this child whom I shall never see again, although he lies concealed in a grown man who bears his name. Across the grass in the fading sunlight he ran, short legs pumping, under the trees, up a hill, then swooping back toward us, head erect, eyes partially closed. In spirit I was running with him, feeling the things he felt; and I was suddenly aware that the child who had escaped my grip and left me would never return. In a brief moment of time his babyhood ended and his boyhood had begun. I could feel time ticking away. My dad, I think, felt it too when he said, "It's such a big field, and he's such a little boy."

And so we said goodbye to a toddler named Tom that day and hello to a boy; and, as the years have rolled on, the experience of greeting and farewell has become a familiar one. I am increasingly more understanding of what my dad meant when he once told me that a parent has so little time.

"Children are young for such a few years," he said. He was looking at me but seeing the boy I had been – a boy who had vanished like smoke, leaving only the memories in his mind and mine. Every child is a will-o'-the-wisp whom clumsy parents try to grasp and hold tight, in vain. My little sister who used ride on my dad's shoulders is gone, and in her place there is the mother of three grown sons. Her children who once held my hand for confidence now walk in places where I cannot follow.

Once each summer my brother and I used to challenge our father to a race. It became a sort of primitive rite, a ceremony, a test. The first year dad easily outran us, for his legs were so much longer. But the following summer dad had to try harder; the next year, harder still. One year dad finished one step ahead.

The following summer the issue went unchallenged. My legs were as long as my father's and my brother wasn't far behind. We all knew, although we did not confess it to one another that we boys had finally won. In a way we could sense that dad was glad, and he was proud of us. And in a way, we were sorry. For in his heart every boy knows he must always try to outdistance his father; but when it happens he knows he has lost as well as gained.

Yesterday I walked with my brother and his son in the woods, shuffling through the fallen leaves, following the trail past a fallen oak and the remnants of a stone wall erected by men now dead. In the field beyond the woods a single crow silently flew away. The wind from the north was cold.

"I like it, even this time of year," my nephew said. He looked up at me, and then away. "Even when I'm old. . ." I waited. ". . . Even when I'm older, we can still come here, can't we, Uncle Bob?" "Yes," I said. "No matter how old you get, we'll walk here like this."

My nephew is already changing into a mature college student who bears his name, then into a man who will stroll through autumn leaves with children of his own. And still, while our memories remain, the woods will live in us as they were the day we stood there and listened to the tick of the passing of time.

Before Winter Comes

There is an old saying, "Opportunity knocks but once." That is not true. Opportunity knocks many times. It is true, however, that opportunity has a way of knocking for the last time. We must take advantage of opportunities before winter comes or lose them forever.

A man was held in the bondage of alcohol. One night he was in his hotel room when his craving came upon him. He reached for the phone to summon a bell boy. Suddenly he seemed to hear a voice. It was saying, "This is your hour. Yield now and it will destroy you. Conquer it now, and you are its master forever." Such moments come to every person. There are decision times and, if allowed to pass by, they are gone forever.

"Before winter comes." As a child we used this phrase when we wanted to put something off, something that we didn't want to do. Adults plan on being dutiful parents to their children. But parents need to get established in business; there is work to do, golf games, dinner meetings, and the desire to sleep late on weekends. The list is endless. Wouldn't it be wonderful if we could put our children in a "time bubble" and keep them there until we were ready for them? Children have a habit of growing up and getting away. If we are going to love our children fully, it must be "before winter comes."

Suppose there are ill feelings between you and a friend. Maybe that person caused the friction. Maybe you did. Maybe the fault is with neither of you. We all know life is too short for that sort of thing. We mean to settle it, but we keep putting it off. Eventually it will have gone too far, or it will be too late. We need to settle it before winter comes.

Whittier was right:
"For of all sad words of tongue or pen,
The saddest are these: 'It might have been!'"

Create a Better World

The winter comes; opportunity has knocked for the last time.

Recently a donor to Hospice called and told me that he wanted to make a $1,000 gift to our non-profit immediately. He said, "I need to do it now. Quick, quick, before my heart gets hard." That's why the Bible speaks of giving "upon the first day of the week." I know people who intended to give, but they held onto their wealth until they had lost their willingness. Do it before winter comes.

I am one who believes that belonging to a church, participating in a civic club, and volunteering for a non-profit organization are all important. I am always amazed at how many people always intend to join a church or a civic club or to become an active volunteer but never seem to get around to it. The years are slipping by. Do it before winter comes.

Winter is a time when it gets cold. Instead of growing, the leaves on the trees turn brown and die. Winter also comes to the human heart. There are many decisions to be made before winter comes.

Usefulness

One of the fundamental laws of life is that only useful things survive evolution. Squirrels have bushy tails because they are useful for balancing on the limbs of trees. Dogs and cats have eyes in the front of their heads because they are hunters and need to keep the game they chase in sight. Rabbits have eyes on the side of their heads because they are not hunters but are hunted, and they need to watch in every direction for approaching enemies. The things we use for our good, we also keep.

The animals have a marvelous sense of smell but people are losing theirs. Animals use theirs for survival but humans increasingly depend on other senses. And that which we do not use eventually dies. Put your arm in a tight sling, keep it inactive, and after a while it will wither. There are fish in Mammoth Cave that are totally blind. They still have eyes but the species has lived in total darkness so long the species no longer has the need for sight.

And so it is with human life. I believe no person is here by accident. Surely we believe the purpose of every life is to be fruitful. And if people fail in their mission they tend to wither and die. Study, as I have so many times, the lives of people who are "fed up" with living and you will find that they are failing to bear any real fruit. You never live until you begin to live for something.

I once spent nearly a week in a small hermitage far back in the mountains. I never enjoyed anything in my life as much as I enjoyed the first two days there. I went to bed at dark and slept for ten hours. I sat on the porch and was awed by the beautiful mountains. I was several miles from a phone and no cell phone. No newspaper was delivered to my door. Nobody came around to see me. There was no mail to answer.

But after a couple of days I caught up on my sleep and I got restless. I walked around through the woods, but just walking without going anywhere didn't appeal to me very long. I wanted something to do. I wanted to be with other people.

I don't know how long I will live. But one thing I do know, I am living now. And that is more than some people can say. I once buried a young soldier who was killed while leading his men in combat. His mother was crushed that he had died so young. But I pointed out to her that he probably packed more real living into that final fight than some people experience in a lifetime.

The unhappiest people in the world are the ones who are living within themselves and useful to no one else I sympathize with the little boy who was so lonely he said to his mother, "I wish I were two little puppies so I could play together."

Let's stop, be still for a moment, and ask ourselves this question: "Is there a single soul who would look us square in the eye and say, 'I thank God for you. My life is better because of you. I am glad you are living.' Would anybody say that to me?" If you were to die tonight, would it be much of a loss to anybody. Would it really?

What is the answer to the fruitless life? Before we do our best, we must first be our best.

Create a Better World

PART THREE – Affirmative Living

The Four Dimensions of Life

There are four dimensions of life (length, breadth, depth, and height) that we must consider as we take advantage of continued learning. We begin to develop personal power and wisdom by consciously opening our minds and being receptive to the countless wonders that abound.

One dimension of life is length, and all people live in that dimension. In response to the question, "How long do you want to live?" I always reply, "As long as I can."

Many years ago a minister, driving in his buggy along a lonely country road, overtook a young man walking along that road. He stopped and invited him to ride. As they were riding along the minister thought to himself that he had not said anything to this young man about his soul, so in a deep, ministerial voice he said, "Young man, are you prepared to die?" As the young man went over the back wheel of the buggy, he shouted back, "Not if I can help it."

We read in the Bible, "And all the days of Methuselah were nine hundred sixty and nine years: and he died" (Genesis 5:27). This is the longest life recorded in all history and the shortest biography. The Bible says nothing bad about Methuselah, but neither does it say anything good. Here was a man who just lived. As far as we know he never did any harm, but neither do we know of any good that he did. Methuselah is a monument to living to a ripe old age. However merely living a long time is certainly not the primary goal in life. Other dimensions of life are far more important.

We need the dimension of "breadth" and taking advantage of continued learning can help us understand and sympathize with the people on this earth and our many differences. However, three things remain the same the world over: a smile, a tear, and a drop of blood. Those three things represent the most important emotions of humankind. When we come to know each other and understand each other, then we find ourselves concerned about each other.

We walk through the fog of ignorance, and as we look at each other from a distance we see monsters and enemies, but when we get close we see brothers and sisters. Living in the dimension of breadth, one is concerned about other people. Are we our brother's or sister's keeper? The answer is, "Emphatically, yes." We cannot live just for the sake of living. We are part of the fellowship with others on this earth.

The third dimension of life is "depth." If you plan to build a tall building, you dig down to form a strong foundation. Every life must be built on foundations. That is the dimension of depth. Unless one develops convictions about life to act as their personal foundation, sooner or later that person's life will be blown apart by the winds of change and the need to make informed decisions that coincide with their value system. Friends, reputation, education, skills, all of these form foundations for living.

On the other hand, if the only thing we had were a foundation, a building would never rise up into the sky. The foundation makes possible the heights, which leads us to our fourth dimension.

In the life dimension of "height" we find our dreams, our hopes, our goals, our ambitions, and our ideals. The phrase, "Hitch your wagon to a star" is good advice. People cannot live rich full lives without their dreams. Once someone asked a mountain climber how he maintained his strength in climbing the mountain, and his reply was, "I keep looking up." Look up and reach for the highest peaks of your life.

Often people come to me with problems. I counsel them and help them to seek higher ground. Many times the problem is potential that hasn't been tapped. By walking right up to the problem with confidence we can work through the four dimensions of life to create something new.

Hallmarks for Living

If you're ever at the seashore, take a moment and watch the tide go out and the tide come in. There is no power on earth great enough to stop the tide, and that principle operates all through life: what goes out comes in. Send out love, and love comes back. Send out hate, and hate comes back. Send out mercy, mercy comes back. What we give, we get.

A psychologist was busy diagnosing a group of sick people. After a thorough examination, he discovered they were full of poisons that would not only eventually destroy their bodies, but rob them of the joy and peace of life while struggling with their illness and eventually would destroy their souls. They were filled with the poisons of envy, jealousy, selfishness and hate. All thought of themselves as more important than any of the others. One claimed to be the finest public speaker. Another insisted she could look into the future, while another felt she was better educated than the others. Still another professed to do more ministries for other people.

The wise doctor told them no matter what abilities they may possess or what services they may render, if their hearts are not filled with love, they did not amount to anything. Then he wrote each of them this prescription of love.

Love is not a single thing, but a complex composite of many things as found in an often cited passage in Chapter thirteen of St. Paul's first letter to the Corinthians.

1) Love is patient. This is the attitude of love. To be patient means to possess endurance under stress or annoyance. Love works today while it waits for tomorrow. On the desk of a very fine businessman I saw the motto, "This, too, shall pass." He told me that that motto had saved him many times. No matter how bad the storm may be, if you are sure that

one day it will blow over and the sun will shine again, you will never give up. Love waits patiently without complaining.

2) Love is kind. That is the activity of love. Many years ago I learned a little verse by Ella Wheeler Wilcox that has been a constant inspiration to me.

> So many gods, so many creeds,
> So many paths that wind and wind,
> When just the art of being kind
> Is all this sad world needs.

A man once said about his sick wife, "There is nothing I would not do for her." One of the neighbors replied, "That is just the trouble. You have been doing nothing for her for 40 years."

3) Love does not envy. Envy leads to hate and hate destroys a soul. Love does not envy because it is a spiritual quality while envy is based on materialism and self-absorption. I have never heard of a person who was envious of another person's goodness.

4) Love is humble. Love and conceit are contradictory terms. All of us need to be small enough to be used. Love takes a towel, girds itself, and gets on its knees to do a menial task that lesser folks are too big to do.

5) Love is courteous. Love possesses tact and good manners. The old, old saying is still true: "Politeness is to do and say, the kindest thing in the kindest way." Love never wants to offend, it never demands its rights, and it is respectful and is ever mindful of the desires and comforts of others.

6) Love does not seek itself. Love is always more concerned with what it can give than with what it can get. Love is seeking to minister rather than to be ministered to. Love understands that it is, "Not what

we gain but what we give, that measures the worth of the life we live."

7) Love is good-tempered. There are people who brag about their temper as if it were a great asset. But it is no credit to be able to get mad. There are two types of sins – the sins of the body and the sins of the disposition; both are bad but of the two, I would rather be in the company of some prodigal who went to the far country than some elder brother who stayed at home and lived a mortal life yet had a bad disposition. Love knows how to keep angry emotions cool and strives to live in harmony with others.

8) Love is not suspicious and never accuses merely on rumor. Love believes the best of every person until proven wrong. And if a person does go wrong, love is not secretly glad and does not gossip about it. Love always congratulates.

9) Love bears all things; Love bears its burdens with dignity, continues to believe, never loses hope and endures to the end. Love is the one thing that will last; no matter what happens and even when everything else is gone.

Sometime the choice boils down to this, if I follow the pathway of love, I must take the chance of not living for myself, but living for others. Can I afford to take that chance? Or must I put my own needs and interests first? I answer that with the assurance that you can stake your life on love.

Pathways to Tranquility

How can you have tranquility in your life? Here are eleven pathways everyone can take to find such harmony.

1) **When something in the past is worrying you, decide whether or not you can do anything about it.** If it is something you can do something about, then do it. Maybe it means making an apology; maybe you should see to the payment of a debt. On the other hand, don't ruin your life today because of the impossibility of doing anything about yesterday. Recently I had a long talk with a man who is destroying his life because he spoke unkindly to his mother. Now she is dead, and he can do nothing about it. Don't destroy yourself needlessly.

2) **Practice forgetting.** I say *practice* because it is not easy, and actually no person ever completely forgets. My goal is to forget the things which are behind me and reach out to the things ahead.

3) **When you are upset and churning inside, make promises very sparingly.** Sometimes under stain and stress we promise a lot more than we need to or ought to and may not be able to deliver. Most promises should be made in a spirit of calmness and peace.

4) **When you are feeling depressed, keep an open mind on the debatable questions.** That is, plan to talk calmly, to think but not to argue. To disagree is not bad, but under the strain and stress that many people feel, disagreement can lead to permanent damage. Oftentimes the settlement of an argument can lead to peace; but more often, efforts to settle an argument under stress lead to disaster.

Create a Better World

5) One if the greatest words to learn is **imperturbability**. That means that no matter what happens, you are going to be calm and peaceful. You are not going to let outside events destroy you inside.

6) **Remember that today is not the last day that you are going to live.** There is also a tomorrow, and you do not have to get everything done and settled today. Affirm your faith in the future by setting aside tasks that can wait and spend time with family or friends. Refresh yourself and know you will be ready for tomorrow.

7) **At night when you come in from a day's work before you sit down to dinner, go and wash your hands.** At the same time practice washing out of your mind the unhappy thoughts and experiences of that day. It is a moment of time to empty your mind of negative feelings so that you can enjoy the rest of the day.

8) Every so often, you need to stop by a filling station and fill up the gasoline tank of your car. Otherwise you car will stop running. So it is with the human mind; **we need to practice filling our minds with those positive thoughts that lead to courage and calmness and joy.** Too many of us find ourselves in a funk because we did not stop to fill up our mind's tank.

9) **Do not waste your worries.** Let your worries become the stimulus for positive action. One of the main purposes of worry is to make us get up and get going in a positive way. If you are stuck by worry, do something. There are times when we do need to be still and quiet, and in those moments we gain strength. But strength is to be used in action. Get busy doing something

positive using the strengths you have built up in less stressful times.

10) **Change your concerns from being self-centered and make them other-centered.** When we become outreaching in our attitudes and in our actions, marvelous blessings return to us. Again and again people have found peace by becoming absorbed in the requests of someone in greater need.

11) **Develop the art of praise, instead of criticism.** Oftentimes when we correct somebody, we try to make ourselves believe that we are interested in helping that person. But most of the people who pick out flaws in other people are only expressing their own insecurity. Start praising other people, and you will find your own inner critic diminishing.

When you take all of your troubles and face up to them in the most practical and reasonable way, you will find true tranquility.

Treat Each Other Well

A mother praying for her child in trouble, youth visiting nursing home residents, one friend rejoicing over another's accomplishment, children saving their allowance for their father's birthday, a husband showing appreciation for his wife's special efforts, a wife comforting her husband at a time of failure – all of these are expressions of treating each other well. They answer the question "what is love" better than any dictionary definition because love defies definition.

I have talked with many people who are literally starving for love. They are bitter and resentful wanting what they see in others around them. Some exhibit the spirit of Frederick the Great, who struck one of his subjects with a whip and exclaimed: "Confound you: I want you to love me." But love is not something which can be commanded.

A definition of love which won a nationwide newspaper contest years ago read: "Love is the doorway through which the human soul passes from selfishness to service and from solitude to kinship with all creation." How we treat people, the service we render to others, is one of the most important lessons of life and our passageway to love.

When I was in seminary, our theology professor gave us a pop quiz. I was a conscientious student and had breezed through the questions until I read the very last one. It read, "What is the name of the woman who cleans the school?" Surely this was some kind of joke. I had seen the cleaning woman hundreds of times. She was tall, short-haired, and in her 50's, but how would I know her name?" I turned in my paper, leaving the last question blank. Just before class ended, one of my classmates asked if the last question counted in our grade. "Absolutely," said our teacher, "In your life you will meet many people. All of them are significant. They deserve your attention and care, even if all you do is say 'hello'." I never forgot that lesson. After the test, I also learned her name was Penny.

I heard a powerful story about treating others well concerning an older African American woman in the early 1960s that was standing on the side of an Alabama highway trying to endure a lashing rainstorm. It was approaching midnight, her car had broken down and she desperately needed a ride. Soaking wet, she decided to flag down the next car. A young white man stopped to help her, generally unheard of in those conflict-filled times. The man took her to safety, helped her get assistance and put her into a taxi. She seemed to be in a big hurry, but wrote down his address and thanked him.

Seven days had gone by when the man heard a knock on his door. To his surprise, a giant color TV was delivered to his home. A special note was attached:

"Thank you so much for assisting me on the highway the other night. The rain drenched not only my clothes, but also my spirits. Then you came along. Because of you, I was able to make it to my dying husband's bedside just before he passed away. God bless you for helping me and unselfishly serving others." Sincerely, Mrs. Nat King Cole

A hospice nurse told me another wonderful story of caring when she worked as a volunteer at a hospital years ago. She said she got to know a little girl who was suffering from a rare and serious disease. The child's only chance of recovery appeared to be a blood transfusion from her five year old brother, who had miraculously survived the same disease and had developed the antibodies needed to combat the illness. The doctor explained the situation to her little brother and asked the little boy if he would be willing to give his blood to his sister. He looked up at the doctor and asked with a trembling voice, "Will I start to die right away?" Being so young, the little boy had misunderstood the doctor. He thought he was going to have to give his sister all of his blood to save her. Yet he was willing to give when it really counted.

There is only one way to make up for the love you have missed. That is through treating others well. Try it. Try it today. Think of someone who irritates you, someone you do not like. Pray for that person right now, stating their name in your prayer. During the day, study that person. What are some of his good qualities? What are some of his bad qualities? Be an amateur psychologist and analyze those traits in the person that cause you not to like him. By seeking to understand you will develop compassion.

Treat each other well. You will feel a lot better. Try it and see.

Listen

We are all familiar with the age-old question: "If a tree falls in the woods, and there is no ear to hear it, does it make a sound?" As far as I know, that dilemma has never been finally settled. But we do know that there can be no teaching or learning if there is no one to listen.

Listening is really a difficult process because the average speaker uses about a hundred to a hundred and twenty words a minute. But a listener has the ability to hear between three and four hundred words a minute. With the listener's ability to hear being greater than the speaker's to speak, it is quite possible for the mind to slip off into other lines of thought and lose the words of the speaker altogether. It requires real disciplined concentration to hear while another one speaks.

Another stumbling block to listeners is their preconceived ideas or prejudices. So often, when a speaker expresses an opinion on which the listener is already biased, the listener may automatically switch from the meaning the speaker has given to his or her own point of view.

Also, there are many ways to listen. One can listen passively; that is, hearing, but not paying attention. Or one may listen partially, failing to hear the whole truth. Or one may listen without being interested, and without response. Or one can listen intently, completely grasping the message.

A person who is mistrustful and self-centered has difficulty truly listening to someone else. Suppose someone we are close to wants to be understood by us. We don't hear them on their terms because we are so intensely involved with our own thoughts. So we react to our feelings rather than really hearing what they are saying about their experiences. Or we may be so worried about who is in control that we fail to accept the information we are being offered. Instead we respond with, "Yes, but . . ."

Create a Better World

My wife and I have begun a healthy habit of really listening to one another when I get home each evening before we do anything else. We sit together, get comfortable, have a drink, and truly listen to one another for 15 to 30 minutes before we move on to the tasks at home. True learning we feel comes, like true intimacy, when we listen and have an open mind to one another. As we detach ourselves, separate from our own ego, we hear each other better and grow more intimate.

Being willing to spend time alone, in quiet, is essential to listening. We often fear silence and being alone, and we escape into distractions and busywork. When we sit in silence and allow ourselves to listen, we focus less on our egotistical concerns and more on our Higher Power.

Understanding of our lives grows through listening. By listening, we become aware of needs, feelings, and responses within ourselves which we previously ignored. By knowing ourselves better, we will be more direct and honest with others and more responsive to them by really listening.

Awareness

Several years ago, there was an old Three Stooges comedy routine on TV in which Larry would call out to Moe, "I can't see! I can't see!" Moe would immediately rush to Larry's aid, asking, "Why not?" Larry would then smile and proclaim, "Because I got my eyes closed!" Then, of course, Moe would promptly bop Larry on the head. It is a good idea to pause occasionally to think about what we may not see in our world because our eyes are closed. And preferably we need to do this before we get "bopped" on the head by circumstances!

If you ask yourself the question, "What is awareness?" I believe that one thing you would think about is your possibilities. Experts say that we use only a very small fraction of our brain power. That is also true of our physical power. It also is true of the opportunities available to us.

Awareness means that we begin to realize something of the infinite potential within ourselves. Beyond that, awareness is being sensitive to other people. That is, we come to understand that other person. I think Anne Morrow Lindbergh said it best in these words, "Each man is an island, but all men are connected by a common sea. We therefore are aware of the potentiality of the person, but, are not limited by his own limitation."

We can go even further in believing that total awareness means a capacity to have fellowship with those who have been released from the limitations of this physical life.

People who live alone have more time to be quiet and think. We need to set aside moments to make an effort to be aware, to begin to understand what our eyes behold, to begin to respond to the stimulation of life which is all around us, and to get the message from every situation. Let us all become more aware.

Create a Better World

A great poetess, Miriam Teichner, wrote the following wonderful words:

"God – let me be aware.
Let me not stumble blindly down the ways,
Just getting somehow safely through the days,
Not even groping for another hand,
Not even wondering why it all was planned;
Eyes to the ground unseeking for the light,
Soul never aching for the wild-winged flight,
Please, keep me eager just to do my share.
God, let me be aware.

God, let me be aware.
Stab my soul fiercely with others' pain,
Let me walk seeking horror and stain.
Let my hands, groping, find other hands.
Give me the heart that divines, understands.
Give me the courage, wounded, to fight.
Flood me with knowledge, drench me in light.
Please, keep me eager just to do my share.
God, let me be aware."

My favorite story is about a man whose one consuming passion was to go to heaven. Finally, he died and did go there. An angel took him by the hand and showed him the beautiful sights, the majestic mountains, lovely flowers, gorgeous sunsets, little children playing in the streets. He exclaimed, "Isn't heaven wonderful?" But the angel said, "This isn't heaven, this is the world in which you lived but never saw."

The Power of Stories

I am forever searching for ideas to illustrate a point, to spark passion, or to provoke reflection. If old truths are not dressed up in new clothes, they easily pass by unnoticed. Stories are constantly needed for presentations to arouse interest and hold attention, not forgetting the touch of humor that is always helpful.

The image of our human life as a journey is both ancient and new, having received a renewed emphasis in recent years. We tell stories of the journey to provide meaning and understanding for life and existence. We tell stories to put ourselves and our listeners in touch with life's mysteries. When asked who we are, we share our own story.

I am a collector of stories that have touched my life and others. I tell them to a variety of groups when I speak about positive living or about the hospice experience. Here are a few of my favorites that I hope touch you as they have me.

On drawing the wrong conclusion: There is the story about an old woman who crossed the Mexican border every day on a motor scooter with a sack of sand behind her. The customs officer eventually became suspicious and inquired, "What have you got in that sack?" "Only sand, sir," came the reply. The officer emptied the sack and, indeed, it contained nothing but sand. And so it went on for a month. One day, the officer said to the old woman, "I won't arrest you or say anything to the police, but just tell me: are you smuggling or not?" "Yes," she answered truthfully. "Well, what are you smuggling?" he pressed her. With a smile, she replied, "Scooters."

About hypocrisy and ambition: This is the tale about an architect, who had worked for a large company for many years, who was called in one day by the board of directors and given plans for a fine house to be built in the best quarter of the town. The chairman instructed him to spare no expense, using the finest materials and the best craftsmen.

Create a Better World

As the house began to go up, the architect began to think, "Why hire expensive labor? Why use such costly materials?" So he began to use poor materials and to hire poor quality workmen, and he put the difference in the cost into his own pocket. When the house was finished, it looked very fine on the outside, but it certainly would not last long. Shortly after it was finished, the board of directors held another meeting to which the architect was called. The chairman made a speech, thanking the architect for his long service to the company, as a reward for which they were making him a present of the house!

About gossip: I love the story of several ministers from a small town who were out fishing in a boat. As the fish weren't biting, they fell to talking. Since they had counseled their parishioners for many years that confession is good for the soul, they decided they would practice what they had been preaching. Each decided to confess his secret sin to the others. The first said that his great fault was language; he still had trouble once in a while holding back improper words. The second minister admitted that his weakness was materialism; he was too fond of money and it was his first and main consideration in changing pastorates. The third preacher broke the news of an addiction to petty gambling on anything from golf to football. The last minister, who was the helmsman of the small craft, had, by this time, turned the boat toward shore and had increased the speed. One of the confessors said, "What's the hurry? Besides you haven't made your confession." The minister replied, "Well, you see, my sin is gossip, and I just can't wait to get home."

On the value of questioning: The story is told about a father and his son who were out walking one afternoon when the youngster asked how electricity went through the wires stretched between telephone poles. "I don't know," said the father. "I never knew much about electricity." A few blocks farther on the boy asked what caused lightning and thunder. "To tell the truth," said the father, "I never understood that myself." The boy continued to ask questions throughout their stroll, none of which the father could answer. Finally, as they were nearing their home, the boy said, "Dad, I hope you don't mind me asking so many questions." "Of course not," replied the father. "How else are you going to learn?"

Stories can capture the imagination, challenge, enlighten, provoke, instill values or deeply disturb people. They are ideally suited for teaching, preaching, personal reflection, humor, and prayer.

Like pictures, stories are worth a thousand words. They have terrific power, especially when savored. Heed my warning: listen, reflect and wonder, and these stories will yield their wisdom.

Life's Great Moments

A woman told me the other day that one of the most memorable experiences of her life happened one cold, rainy morning just about daylight. She said she stood on a street corner and watched her oldest son get on a bus and head out for an army camp and the war. She said she watched the bus until it was out of sight. She said she would never forget that moment.

Many people have experienced similar moments in their own lives. Their plans have been interrupted, and the things they wanted to do had to be put aside. Through no fault of their own, circumstances were such that they had to go into a life that they did not want, that they dreaded, and even feared. It was not an easy time.

It is interesting to make a list of the great moments of your life. Such a list could be long. Let me suggest some of the things that come to mind. I remember when I became a member of the first team in junior college basketball and I was not a substitute any longer. Going out to start the game was a thrilling experience. When I graduated from college, preached my first sermon, got married, accumulated a few extra dollars in a savings account, these were great moments and the list goes on.

Then I think of the lives of other people. Most of the things that were great moments for me have not been experienced by others. This is especially true of people who lived centuries ago or who currently live in third world countries or even a fellow worker.

All of us have days when we may feel cheated in life. When that happens, it's good to make a list of the great things in our life that other people never experience. This past Thanksgiving a Rotary friend sent me such a list which I have abbreviated:

- If you woke up this morning with more health than illness – you are more blessed than the million who will not survive this week.
- If you have never experienced the danger of battle, the loneliness of imprisonment, the agony of torture, or the pangs of starvation – you are ahead of 500 million people in the world.
- If you can attend a church meeting without fear of harassment, arrest, torture, or death – you are more blessed than three billion people in the world.
- If you have food in the refrigerator, clothes on your back, and a roof over your head and a place to sleep – you are richer than 75% of the world's population.
- If you have money in the bank, in your wallet, and spare change in a dish someplace – you are among the top 8% of the world's wealthy.
- If you hold up your head with a smile on your face and are truly thankful – you are blessed because the majority can but most do not.
- If you can read this message, you just received a double blessing in that someone was thinking of you, and furthermore, you are more blessed than over two billion people in the world that cannot read at all.

We can start our personal list today. You can begin at any age. Decide to start. You cannot go back and start life over as a baby. You are who you are, and you are the age you are, and you are where you are. Life's great moments await you.

PART FOUR – Prayer and Giving Thanks

Need Finds a Voice

There are many times when I like to be alone, close my eyes, and express to God in words the feelings of my heart. That is prayer. Sometimes I pray as I am walking along the street or driving my car. I don't close my eyes then, though I often speak the words aloud. At other times I pray when I am in a group and don't care to express my thoughts through speech. Though kneeling, eyes closed, and an expression of words may be helpful in prayer, one can pray without the use of these aids.

I say this to point out that many of us have limited prayer to specific times, like in church or Temple or at night before bed. Many times the exercise of prayer is an experience not related to our every day lives. It's something we do apart from the rest of our lives. We draw aside, use language which is not normal, go through the act of formal prayer, and then get back into the stream of our busy lives.

For us, prayer may be like the experience of religion for a man I met long ago. He had a nice suit which he wore only on Sunday. On those mornings he would put on the suit, go to church, come home, pull off his suit, and go about his business. That was his religious practice. It was something completely unrelated to his life.

Like religion, prayer is more fulfilling when it involves all of life. Our whole life can be a prayer. Every thought, every feeling, every act can be prayer. Communication in my marriage involves far more than the conversations my wife and I have when we're together. We talk a lot, but there are times when I may be a thousand miles away from home. Even then everything I say and do involves us both. I am married to her all of the time, not only when we are conversing in person. God is not divorced from me at any time and neither am I ever divorced from God. God is within me and in all that I do. Life is prayer.

Expression of prayer takes many forms. It may be in the form of speech, or as a poet once said, "the soul's sincere desire." Truly the deep longing of our hearts is prayer, whether we express it in words or not. In fact, it may be that the unconscious longings are some of our strongest prayers.

Prayer is fellowship with God. Prayer is seeking to understand one's self. The height of spiritual experience has been reached by many by honestly facing our true selves. Prayer is self-discipline which comes as a result of discovering God's will and then making the necessary adjustments in feelings and actions. The height in prayer comes as a result of the co-mingling of human desire and God's will. Certainly for me prayer is in every relationship I hold dear. It's in all my ambitions, in all my activities; it is in all of my life.

Prayer has become part of my attitude, not only as an occasional act. Prayer is constant fellowship, not just the saying of words – although the occasional act and the saying of words may be used as steps toward a constant prayerful attitude and fellowship.

Prayer is need finding a voice. a friend in search of a friend. Prayer is speaking, or thinking, or feeling with the belief that there is One who hears, who cares and who will respond. George Meredith said, "Who riseth from prayer a better man, his prayer is answered." That is really the best result of prayer, but prayer brings definite and tangible results. However, we must keep in mind that we ourselves must become part of the answer.

Here is an illustration: A poor man who lived in the country had an accident and broke his leg. That meant he was laid up for a long while, unable to work. His family was large and needed help. Someone got up at a prayer meeting at the church to pray for this family. While the people were praying and asking God to help the family, there was a loud knock on the door of their home. Someone tiptoed to the door, opened it, and there stood a young farm boy who said, "My dad could not attend the prayer meeting tonight, so he just sent his prayers in a wagon." And there was the wagon loaded with potatoes, meat, apples, and other things from the farm. There was an instance where prayers were loaded in a wagon.

As I said, we must become part of the answer to our prayers, but only part. God adds to our abilities, opportunities, and resources whatever is needed and is right to bring about the full answer. It is as Tennyson said,

> "More things are wrought by prayer
> Than this world dreams of . . . ."

Pray for One Another

All of us have times we feel helpless. Our loved one is beyond our reach. Someone is desperately sick. A situation at work seems hopeless. In times like this it is good to know we can pray. Not only is praying for others our privilege, it is our solemn duty.

Praying for another person helps them and it helps the person who prays. A man spoke to me one day about a neighbor who had done him a great wrong. Rather defiantly he said, "Don't preach to me about forgiveness. I can't forgive him and even if I could, I wouldn't." I replied, "I only ask you to do one thing: pray for him."

When we pray for a loved one who needs help, we nurture a spirit of hope and optimism that becomes important in our own lives. When your child is sick, you feel a great sense of relief when the doctor comes because you know he can do something. And when you lift someone who needs help into the hands of God, you feel peace in your heart knowing God can do something. Praying for someone else helps you.

When we know there is someone praying for us, that very knowledge is a source of sustaining strength. I know a lot of people who are praying for me, and to each one I am deeply grateful. All of us are helped by knowing someone is praying for us.

When I pray for someone, it inspires me to do what I can to help that person. Quite often the effort of the person praying is enough to answer the prayer. For example, suppose I pray for someone who is sick. It may be that a contributing factor in that sickness is that the person is lonely, discouraged and has lost the will to live. As a result of my praying, I am moved to acts of thoughtfulness and kindness which may change my friend's mental attitude, possibly becoming his turning point from illness to health.

Praying for another person includes five easy steps:

1) **Pray specifically for that person.** Get the person clearly in your mind so that you can see him or her vividly. Decide as definitely as you can the need of that person, considering the circumstances of his or her life.

2) **Holding that particular person in mind, think of God.**

3) **Think of your prayer as lifting that person into the presence of God.** You are not trying to tell God something He does not know. Neither are you trying to persuade God to do something He doesn't want to do. Realize, as St. Augustine said, "Without God, we cannot; without us, God will not." Think of yourself as supplying the human cooperation that is necessary to bring the person and God together.

4) **Tell God what is in your heart.** Remember, however, to pray positively. Don't concentrate on the person's weakness, sickness, or wrong. Rather, concentrate on the person's strengths and picture in your mind the answer you want and picture that person receiving that answer. Pray hopefully.

5) **Keep praying until God's answer comes.**

Picture a person in one room of a house and God in the next room. Between the two there is a wall. But if you stand in the doorway connecting the two rooms, then you can see them both. One could speak to the other through you. It may be that you have contact with someone who needs God's help. There may be a wall between God and that person. It may be a wall of disbelief, unconcern, or wrong living. But because you have contact both with that person and with God, you become the intermediary between the two and your prayers connect that person's need with God's power. This is intercessory prayer.

Pray for one another.

Daring to Ask

My wife Kathy and I went to Hawaii for our honeymoon. One of the best things we did then was to buy a time share on Poipu Beach on the garden island of Kauai. Every three years we put our weeks together and return for three weeks in paradise.

Every morning at sunrise and every evening at sunset we go out to the beach and watch the water. It's always a spiritual experience. I become acutely conscious of the deep silence of nature. The quietness is such that I can hear my heart beating, and I notice the steady undeviating rhythm.

As I feel my heart beating, I turn my eyes and look through the sea grass near me. I notice how clean it has been washed by the tides. Also, I notice that the grass moves slowly and gracefully to and fro with the gentle breeze. As I watch I become conscious that the grass, too, has a rhythm, like the rhythm of my heart.

Then my eyes lift to the ocean and I watch the waves rise and fall and roll up onto the clean sand. I become aware that it, too, has a rhythm, a rhythm like the waving of the grass and the beating of my heart. I realize that there is a fundamental harmony throughout the universe. I realize that I am in tune with nature and I realize that God is the Creator, and that I am in tune with God.

There I see the beginning of prayer, the becoming attuned and connected with God, the source of all strength and power. There is no need to turn on the switch, seeking the blessings of prayer, until our lives have become properly allied with God.

James M. Barrie wrote, "The reason birds can fly and we can't is simply that they have perfect faith, for to have faith is to have wings." That is, if we have the faith, we will somehow get the means to carry out that faith. The Wright brothers did have faith that we could fly and they developed the wings. When we ask God with faith, immediately we rid our minds of our destructive negative thoughts and we begin to develop a marvelous confidence, a threefold confidence.

1. We develop confidence in ourselves. People who have lost their nerve are unfortunate creatures. They shrink from every task and turn away from every opportunity. But when they believe in themselves, they develop power and strength they did not know they had. However, we must remind ourselves that confidence in ourselves is not enough. It is good as far as it goes but it doesn't go far enough.

2. When we believe in ourselves, we develop faith in our friends. We need the support of each other. Why do men and women marry? It isn't just the physical relationship. Human beings have needs deeper than physical needs and true faith leads us to believe in the goodness and reliability of other people, and to draw strength from our friendships. But we also have needs that others cannot meet.

3. Faith not only leads us to self-confidence and confidence in other people, it also leads us to confidence in God. So for the person of faith, the philosophy of life, "Try asking God," has great meaning. The best definition of prayer I know is that "prayer is an offering up of our desires unto God for things agreeable to His will." That puts the center of prayer where it belongs, not on the things we ask for, but rather upon God and God's will. The true purpose of prayer should not be getting from God, but giving ourselves to God.

Someone once asked me to describe my philosophy of life. My philosophy has been simply, "To try asking God." I seek to practice this philosophy when I'm in trouble, in need, in disappointment, and in every circumstance of my life.

One Heart and One Soul

Put a tray of ice cubes into a bowl. At first, each cube is separate from the others. But as they begin to warm up, they melt together into one pool of water. This typifies what happens when a team or a community jells. When the spirit of teamwork happens within a group, it becomes one heart and one soul. The group becomes united into an unbroken fellowship. When people get this spirit, they will give 100 percent. Also, the reverse is true: when people start giving, they develop this spirit of teamwork.

The people most of us dislike the most are the "What's in it for me?" folks. These "me-first" people won't feel warmth coming from others. You never find happiness when your favorite charity is yourself. The people who forget themselves while thinking of others are the ones who say, "Let's go!" They never lack fellowship and friendship. The "me-first" people are the ones who always end up being left out of a fellowship of community.

Too many times we blame other people for our mistakes. When we are alone and lonely, it is too easy to say that everybody else marched off in the wrong direction, and we were the only ones to go the right way.

The strengthening power of fellowship is really worth it. I often say to people who join an organization, "It takes only a little time to put your name on the roll, but to really become a member of this organization will take longer. It requires working with the people and becoming one of the many." Fellowship with others requires the giving of much, but eventually the getting of much more.

There was a university professor who searched for the meaning of life. After several years and many miles, he came to the hut of a holy hermit and asked to be enlightened. The holy man invited his visitor into his humble dwelling and began to serve him tea. He filled the pilgrim's cup and then kept on pouring so that tea was soon dripping onto the floor.

The professor watched the overflow until he could no longer restrain himself. "Stop! It is full. No more will go in." "Like this cup," said the hermit, "you are full of your own opinions, preconceptions, and ideas. How can I teach you unless you first empty your cup?"

To have the feeling and reality of one heart and one soul we must do two things: empty ourselves and really be willing to share.

A little girl was sent to the corner store with specific instructions from her mother to come directly home after her purchases. She was gone over two hours, much to the distress of her anxious mother. "Where have you been?" scolded her mother. "I'm sorry, Mommy. I know I am late, but Jane broke her doll and I had to stop and help her fix it" the child answered. "And how could you help her fix that broken doll?" her mother replied.

In her precious, childlike manner the girl responded, "I really couldn't, but I sat down with her and helped her cry."

The power of fellowship and community brings new optimism and joy. We have been to football games and have seen a stadium full of people who rise to their feet, clap their hands, and shout at the top of their lungs. We have seen the same things happen after a performance by a great symphony orchestra. I have heard people say they were so moved by the feeling of community that "their cup runneth over." One woman even said that she was so happy that not only did her cup runneth over, but her saucer, too.

When we become one heart and one soul, coldness and indifference are melted away, enthusiasm takes over, the warmth of love permeates our emotions, and our beliefs become living forces.

Words We Live By

One of the joys of my life has been the opportunity to speak to various groups about "Positive Living," "Inner Peace," and similar topics. Along the way I have met some wonderfully generous individuals who shared articles, books, and quotes they knew I would enjoy. I recently received the 1947 classic "Words to Live By." This book was published at a time when Americans were readjusting from wartime conditions to the uneasy terms of atomic peace.

Reading "Words to Live By" has made me realize there are many things that have never changed. The law of gravity is the same as it was in the beginning. The four seasons come and go as they always have. The tides of the oceans rise and fall. Human feelings, hopes, fears, sorrows, and happiness are the same today as they have been through the centuries.

I have talked with enough people of all ages to come to the conclusion that the three greatest desires of humankind are to be loved, to feel secure, and to feel important. Most of those people put "feeling important" as the greatest desire of their lives. We all want to feel that we are counting for something; we want meaning for our lives.

A number of my friends have collections of quotes and sayings we often use for inspiration. "Words To Live By" was conceived as a collection of such quotes and sayings combined with the actual experience of the people who chose them. The following have been an inspiration to me and have all come from this tome:

> "Only one person in a thousand knows the
> trick of really living in the present."
> *-Storm Jameson*

Those who have the fewest regrets are those who take each moment as it comes for all that it is worth. It will never come again, for better or worse. It is ours alone, we can make it what we will.

"The sky is the daily bread of the eyes."

-Ralph Waldo Emerson

The immensity of the sky can turn happiness to exaltation, comfort us in grief and offer the bright intimation of hope or escape. Whenever the world appears to be at its worst, take a look at the wayward splendor overhead. The chances are it will be at its best.

"We must relearn to be alone."

-Anne Morrow Lindbergh from "Gift from the Sea"

Make it a point to stop and take time to make your own acquaintance. You'll probably get something of a surprise. Because you'll be meeting a very nice and stimulating person – yourself!

"It goes on."

-Robert Frost (on his 80th Birthday)

In all the confusions of today, with all our troubles, with politicians and people slinging the word "fear" around, all of us become discouraged, tempted to say this is the end, the finish. But life goes on. It always has. It always will.

"History teaches us to hope."

-Robert E. Lee

There is always in the background a divinity that shapes our endings, an all-wise and all-powerful God, Who has a very mysterious and wonderful way of ringing good out of evil.

"If a man does not make some new
acquaintances, as he advances through life,
he will soon find himself left alone."

-Dr. Samuel Johnson

When the day comes for me to step aside to make room for the younger generation, I want to do it gracefully, without regrets or jealousy. I intend to keep on having a future instead of merely a past.

"Every minute starts an hour."

-Paul Gandola

And every minute is a new opportunity. Each time the clock ticks you have a change to start over, to say, do, think or feel something in such a way that you and the world are the better for it.

"Four simple things to say to yourself each day:
'Fear Nothing.'
'Thank God.'
'Why Worry?'
'All's Well.'"
-*A. P. Herbert*

"Something to ask yourself every day, 'What was the happiest thing that happened today?'"
-*J. Harvey Howells*

Words are not just sounds or written symbols. Our word is a force. It is the power we have to express and communicate, to think, and to create the events of our lives. The words we live by determine the circumstances of our lives.

Create a Better World

My Greatest Blessing

Next to the salvation of my soul and my birth, marrying Kathy was the most important thing and the best thing that ever happened in my life. Our years together have been my greatest blessing.

As I think about marriage (and especially my own marriage) there are three actions that I feel are basically essential to its depth. One is **appreciation**. Kathy and I make each other feel appreciated. I once asked a woman on her 50th Wedding Anniversary, "How did you hold the love of your husband?" Her reply was very wise: "Learn a hundred ways of saying, 'I think you are wonderful.'" Kathy does that and I'll love her for it until I die.

I feel **perseverance** is also important in marriage. When two people marry they should be in love, and that romantic love is thrilling and beautiful. But that first love cannot be compared in strength and quality to the love that is developed through the years as those two people "share each other's woes, bear each other's burdens," as declared in the favorite old hymn "Blest Be the Tie That Binds."

Years ago in Elizabethtown, I heard a boy give a definition of love. I still think it is the best definition I ever heard. He said: "Love is two hearts that yearn for one sweet presence, where his'n is her'n and her'n is his'n."

Love is not enough for marriage. Couples must dream and plan together. They must play and work together. They must spend their money and rear their children together. Little by little, they become one, developing completeness of themselves through perseverance together.

The third action I mention as being so important in marriage is **prayer**. Marriage is a spiritual experience and it must be kept on that plane. Whenever we pray The Lord's Prayer together at church or at home, Kathy and I join hands. The Lord's Prayer begins with God and then it looks out on life with optimistic faith. It believes God's Kingdom will come; that our daily physical needs will be met; that our sins will be forgiven; that we will have strength for the trials of life that lie ahead. It's the perfect prayer.

Kathy and I honor each other with six daily affirmations that guide us:

1) Be liberal with praise. Build each other up! Admire and verbally love one another.
2) Schedule leisurely breaks for conversation.
3) Work and sacrifice is the secret for success.
4) The Golden Rule – Do for your mate what you want for yourself.
5) Live in the present. Enjoy each moment with each other totally.
6) See the God within each other without expecting the other to be God.

Every night before sleep Kathy and I pray for one another. She has been the inspiration of my life through the years, and I thank God for her because only God could have made her just as she is and guided us to find each other.

Create a Better World

Graced

Every person who ever lived on this earth stands in need of grace. Grace is unmerited divine assistance that regenerates us. And there are three ways we need to be graced: mercy, strength, and beauty.

1. **Mercy.** Grace, in this connection, means "the unmerited favor, the mercy, and the loving kindness of our Creator." Grace is the ultimate expression of love – the love that is seeking, selfless, suffering, saving and supreme

Author, Clarence E. McCartney told of a little girl in Scotland who liked to go with her shepherd father and listen as he called the sheep. By and by she grew to womanhood; moved to the city, away from her father; and eventually drifted into a life that led to despair and loneliness.

When word reached her father, the old shepherd went to the city; but he could not find her. One day he started walking the streets, sounding the shepherd's call loud and free. His daughter's heart suddenly leaped. The call was unmistakable. She rushed out into the street and into her father's arms.

That is the experience we sing about in one of the most popular hymns:

> Amazing grace – how sweet the sound –
> That saved a wretch like me!
> I once was lost, but now am found,
> Was blind but now I see.

2. **Strength for Life's Burdens.** The term "thorn in the flesh" sooner or later comes to have meaning for everyone. For John Milton it meant blindness; for Alfred Lord Tennyson it was loneliness; for Jean Francois Millet it was poverty. For each of

us it means something. We pray repeatedly
that our "thorn" might be removed.

On the other hand, we might pray for the grace to bear it.
In that sense grace means "the power to overcome." Think
of an oyster quietly sleeping in the depth of the sea. A tiny
grain of sand is borne along in the current and is caught by
the oyster's open shell. An irritation has entered the oyster;
but instead of fighting the intruder, the oyster proceeds to
manufacture an exudation of gummy substance, which it
spins out around the "thorn in its flesh." Thus the grain of
sand becomes a pearl. A pearl is the garment of patience
which buffers an annoyance.

During World War I, French Cardinal Mercier's beautiful
cathedral was bombed, his priceless books destroyed, and
some of his students slain in cold blood. Out of the
experience that great man of God wrote: "Suffering accepted
and used will give you a serenity which may well prove the
most exquisite fruit of your life."

Milton's blindness resulted in Paradise Lost. Grace
wrought "In Memoriam" out of Tennyson's loneliness, and
The Angelus from Millet's poverty. Or as Lloyd C. Douglas
put it, "Sometimes God doesn't save us from the storm but
in the storm." Grace is the substance God puts around your
thorn, and of it makes the pearl of your life.

3. Graceful Beauty. Here grace means
"charm, beauty and radiance." It is a
marvelous experience for people to become
graceful. It means they are poised,
harmonious, and free of conflict within
themselves and with other people.

Many times my wife and I have visited the mountains and
beaches of various states. One afternoon in the mountains of
Colorado we fixed a picnic lunch and drove to a spot more
than a mile high. The air felt so clean you wanted to breathe
as deeply as possible. The sunshine on the distant peaks
seemed like a halo.

Create a Better World

We climbed a short way down the mountainside to where a little creek tumbled over a big rock, and there we ate our lunch. Food had never tasted so good to me. The stream was clear and cold. In reverent quiet we watched the sun gradually drop out of sight. The very beauty of the world about us was refreshing. The mountains, the trees, the little creek, and rocks cast their spell over us, and I experienced the great grace within them all.

In this sense grace gives us an undisturbed, calm attitude. We develop a sense of easygoingness, and we begin to live on a level above the petty irritations and exasperations.

A lady's dainty handkerchief was ruined by an ugly ink blot. The painter John Ruskin saw it and asked to borrow it for a few days. When he brought it back, where there had been a blot, there was now beauty; for he made the blot the center of a lovely design. This analogy shows how we can make a problem in our lives something beautiful.

Mercy, strength, and beauty are the three marks of grace which make us grateful and kind. They contribute rich threads to our personal tapestry. Being grateful and knowing we are graced influences our attitude; it softens our harsh exterior and takes the threat out of most uncomfortable situations.

Create a Better World

PART FIVE – Death and Dying

Dealing with Challenging Times

When we come to challenging times and we feel like abandoning our ideals, giving up the struggle, and quitting life, it is helpful to ask ourselves some very important questions, such as: Can good be defeated by evil? In view of the change that is coming to my life, is anything left for me? Is there something I can do? Should I just fold my hands and suffer quietly? Can I wait patiently for resolution?

Patience does not mean sitting down and doing nothing. Patience endures today, while it works for tomorrow. Each of us has our own thing, work to do, something to stand for, things that cannot be lost.

On the other hand, since we do live in a world of constant change, impatience is also an attribute to be desired and cultivated. Einstein is said to have attributed his success in his scientific studies to the fact that he "had learned to challenge an axiom."

We all know that an *axiom* is a universally recognized truth, but a few people refuse to accept axioms. Just because a situation is as it is does not mean that it cannot be challenged. Impatience can be one of our greatest assets – the unwillingness to accept things as they are. The more we think about it, the more we understand that *patience* and *impatience* can walk hand in hand through life, giving strength, hope, and victories.

There are at least two things that we can and should do to deal with the tough times:

> **Let's face the situation as it is.** There is an old story of two men who were riding on a train through the outskirts of a large city. One of them reached over and pulled down the shade, saying, "I cannot stand to look at the

sordid conditions of the slum area we are passing through." His companion replied, "It may be there is nothing we can do at the moment about the conditions, but at least we can keep the shade up." So it is in our own lives. Just closing our eyes to the situations as they are is not going to solve any problems. Even though we do not know the answers, we can keep looking at life's situations and recognizing their existence.

Next we need to develop some "self-distrust." To use the word *distrust* here seems paradoxical. But really it is very important and essential. There are times when we need to confess our own failures. There are moments when we need to believe that we are not strong enough. Oftentimes, strengthening humility comes in confessing our own failures. Sometimes our hope for tomorrow is based upon abandoning our self-confidence and self-reliance. Then we are able to look for help and support beyond ourselves.

The power to keep going really begins with recognizing our foibles and failures. Out of recognizing our weaknesses comes a reaching out for strengths and wisdom that is beyond our self. There is a story about pianist Arthur Rubinstein visiting in New York. His host asked him if he would like to attend church on Sunday morning. He replied, "Yes, if you will take me to hear a preacher who will challenge me to do the impossible." As we face the truth of our lives, and as we begin to believe there is a tomorrow and there is help, we take on new life, and maybe even new, thrilling adventures.

Create a Better World

Death – The Final Frontier

Yesterday 200,000 people died. Death, our final frontier, happens in so many ways. Some died angry. Some died confused. Some were suicidal or victims of violence. Many died peacefully, accepting the reality of life and death. Some died with family and friends; others were alone.

We live today in a world heavily preoccupied with death. Schools and colleges offer courses on death and dying. There are drawn-out courtroom debates on a person's right to die. Magazines and television programs report the long discussions of learned people on the subject of death.

As a former chaplain at a Hospice, I have offered spiritual and emotional support to terminally ill patients and their families. As patients contemplate their own deaths, issues that most often surface are the unfinished business of their lives and the unfinished grieving for themselves or a loved one. Most often these issues deal with parents or other family members. I have found that the more "baggage" a person carries, the greater the fear of death.

Death is the ultimate letting go, the complete relaxing. The more we age, the more we must let go. Life is a series of losses, a series of deaths and new beginnings. Within each death is a new understanding. As we die to self and ego throughout our lives, we discover the awe and mystery for all of life.

Guided imagery, meditation, and specific exercises can help seriously ill people. One meditation begins with a multimillion dollar mansion with a spectacular view overlooking the ocean. The mansion's owner invites his best friend to enjoy his estate. The owner is planning a trip to a distant land. He tells his friend he could be gone two months, two years, or 10 years. He can come back any time. The guest is thrilled about this opportunity. He accepts the owner's invitation and enjoys his new home. After five years, the owner returns. The best friend could say, "Why did you come back?" or "Thank you for such a wonderful five years."

The meditation is much like life and death. When confronted with sickness or death, we can have an attitude of either "Why me?" or one of gratitude for what we have enjoyed. The earth is certainly not our true and final home. It is at best a kind of hotel, a hospice, and a wayfarer's inn, from which we shall be discharged or forced to depart, perhaps at the time we least expect.

Death, the dying process, grief and other forms of loss are all teachers and learning opportunities for emotional and spiritual growth. Contemplating death may actually enrich your life. Some of the following exercises will enrich your life by confronting death:

1. What would be your response if God asked you for three good reasons why you should live?

2. If you had control of drawing your life line, how long would you draw it? Where does your current age fit on the life line?

3. Explore your beliefs about death by writing your own obituary.

4. Imagine you are lying on your deathbed. All of the significant people in your life are there. You have an opportunity to speak to each one from your heart. Who are the significant ones? What do you tell them one by one?

5. Write a Loving Will to be read by the significant persons in your life after you have died.

Consider that at each moment of time we have the choice to accept the treasures of eternal wealth. If you were promised all of the money you could count in one day, or all of the land you could walk around in one day, wouldn't you immediately count the money as fast as you could? Do not say that you will do tomorrow what you could do today. For today will then be lost forever, and it will never return.

Taking the Fear from Death

Every one of us is curious about death because we know that some day we are going to die. A lot of people are afraid of death, and their fear takes much of the joy out of their lives. Many refuse to think about it at all. But death is not a monster. It is a friend, and if we could be convinced of that, life would be so much freer and happier.

I remember visiting many folks in the hospital or at home for Hospice who, instead of dreading death, said they looked forward to it as the greatest blessing of their lives. They were not the least bit afraid. There was joy in their hearts and radiance in their eyes.

One of the greatest scientists this world has ever produced is Thomas A. Edison. He was a very exact man and was never satisfied until he had the full and final truth. His statements were always based on proven facts. When Mr. Edison was dying, he was heard to whisper, "It is very beautiful over there." Thomas A. Edison, a genuine scientist and scholar, would never have said that had it not been true. "It is very beautiful over there" – he was reporting what he saw.

As Robert Louis Stevenson came to his last moment on earth, he whispered, "If this is death, it is easy. Alfred Lord Tennyson was convinced that this life is the "dull side of death."

There are many reasons why we should not fear death. First, death is the doorway to a larger life. We hate to leave the associations and interests of this life, but then there is larger life waiting beyond. There is something glorious and joyful about our eternal existence.

Secondly, we need not fear death, because God is God. Think of how wise and tender God is. Since God planned our birth in this world, we can rest assured that God has planned our entrance into the next in some matter that will be even more wonderful.

There are several thoughts that help us when one we love dies. It is good to remember that death itself is not a bad experience. Most human beings not only die like heroes, but, in my experience, die without pain or fear. When we realize that death was really a good experience for our loved one, it helps ease our pain.

Second, it helps that perhaps death was a blessing for our loved one. There are many things worse than death, and I rather think that, instead of becoming harsh and bitter when we have lost a loved one, we might better have faith in the goodness and mercy of God. Only God knows all the facts. Instead of hating God for letting a loved one die, we might later thank God with all our hearts that they are free of suffering.

Someone once wrote a poem about a wild duck. He could fly high and far, but one day he landed in a barnyard. There life was less exciting but easier. The duck began to eat and live with the tame ducks and gradually he forgot how to fly. He became fat and lazy. In the spring and fall, however, as the wild ducks flew overhead, something stirred inside him, but he could not rise to join them. The poem ends with these lines:

"He's a pretty good duck for the shape he's in,
But he isn't the duck that he might have been."

Many people are walking around on this earth. Their hopes are dead. Their dreams and ideals have died and left a lifeless shell, often referred to as the living dead

Once a new highway was being built in England. It was to run between Holborn and the Strand. A very, very old building stood in the way of progress. The workmen tore it down and cleared off the ground on which it stood. After the ground had been exposed to the sunshine and rain for some months, a wonderful thing happened. Flowers began to spring up, and botanists and naturalists from all over England came to study them. Many of the flowers were identified as plants the Romans had brought to England almost 2,000 years before. Hidden there in the ground, without air and light, the seeds seemed to have died. But they were not dead. As soon as the obstacles were cleared away, and the sunshine let in, they sprang into the fullness of their beauty.

So the seeds of eternal life are in every human life. Often those seeds are buried under such things as unbelief, selfishness, pride, lust, preoccupation, or some other sin. Marvelous things happen within our souls when we work to remove our spiritual obstacles and we become finer and better than ever we had dared to hope. Life takes on a new meaning, a new radiance and beauty, a new happiness, and peace becomes ours. We live again.

Create a Better World

PART SIX – Words for the Journey

The Seven Wonders of the World

Once I asked myself, "What are my Seven Wonders of the World?," based on the things I have personally seen. I came up with these:

1. Niagara Falls
2. The Canadian Rockies
3. The Grand Canyon
4. Mont-Saint-Michel in France
5. The Sistine Chapel in Rome
6. The Island of Kauai in Hawaii
7. The California Redwoods

A group of students were asked to list what they thought were the present Seven Wonders of the World. Though there was some disagreement, the following got the most votes:

1. Egypt's Great Pyramids
2. Taj Mahal
3. Grand Canyon
4. Panama Canal
5. Empire State Building
6. St. Peter's Basilica
7. China's Great Wall

While gathering votes, the teacher noted that one quiet student, hadn't turned in her paper yet. So she asked the girl if she was having trouble with her list. The girl replied, "Yes, a little. I couldn't quite make up my mind because there were so many." The teacher said, "Well, tell us what you have, and maybe we can help."

The girl hesitated, then read, "I think the Seven Wonders of the World are to touch, to taste, to see, to hear, to feel, to laugh and to love." The room was so full of silence you could have heard a pin drop.

It is far too easy for us to look at the exploits of humankind and refer to them as wonders while we overlook what God has done for us. Those things we overlook as simple and ordinary are the things that are truly wondrous.

Life is a Journey

Life is a journey.

We cherish the words of our founding fathers and mothers of this nation when they talked about "life, liberty, and the pursuit of happiness." The words "pursuit" and "purpose" go together. If you are in pursuit without purpose, you become "untoward." The word "untoward" is not a word that is used in our modern language. It means not going toward anything – running around in circles – no specific direction – no purpose. "Untoward" means a meaningless existence.

Every stream of water in the world – a branch, a creek, a river – has one purpose. The purpose of every stream on this earth is to flow toward the sea. If the stream stops that pursuit, it becomes a swamp. Likewise, when a life loses its purpose and stops its pursuit short of its goal, it becomes stagnated and stalemated. When life ceases to be a journey, it becomes an unhappy burden. I have known many people who lost respect for themselves, because they felt they had lost their purpose.

> "Build on resolve, and not upon regret,
> The structure of thy future . . .
> Waste no tears upon the blotted record of lost years
> But turn the leaf, and smile . . . Oh, smile, to see
> The fair white pages that remain for thee."
>
> *-Author Unknown*

I have found it a "must" to set daily goals for myself. I have a positive habit of repeating for nine days in the morning one business goal and two personal goals. After nine days I change the three goals and start over. I find that deliberately setting these goals and praying over them makes them reality and guides my journey.

Because life is a journey, we must keep going.

I know of an outstanding lady who ran a home for retired people. She found that many of these people sat around this home bored, doing nothing, and were really missing the joys of life. She worked out what she called a "five-year plan." She would talk to each one of the people about setting a goal that could be reached in five years. She had wonderful results. One lady said that she had always wanted to paint, and as a result of the five-year plan, she took painting lessons and accomplished her dream. A man revealed that his lifelong goal had been to read the New Testament in Greek. The director got in touch with a Greek teacher for him and long before the five years were up, he had literally read the New Testament in Greek. This woman also convinced the residents that you do not have to accomplish all of life's purposes in one effort.

I used to find it very difficult to keep going when someone I loved died or experienced a terrible tragedy. But my mother, being the wise woman she is, sat me down as a teenager and put things in perspective for me. She said, "Wait a minute, son. You must remember that this person never belonged to us in the first place. That we ever got to love them at all was a gift. So instead of being mad at their being taken away, let's use this occasion to be grateful that we had them at all on our journey."

The greatest thing we can do is to remind ourselves that life is a gift – every last moment of it, and that the way to respond for that gift is to be grateful. We must keep going. We must keep our eyes on the purpose.

Unlocking the Mystery

One of the characters in *Alice in Wonderland* is a lock. I presume it was an ordinary padlock. This lock was very restless. It could not be still even for a moment. It was always running around looking behind every stone, stump, and tree. It was always hunting for something. As Alice watched it, her curiosity was aroused, and she asked, "What is the matter?" The lock replied, "I need something to unlock me."

Some people's measure of success is how much they can grab hold of and hold on. As I go about I see a lot of "coffin" people. They remain locked up, having room in their lives for themselves and nobody else. They fail to unlock the mystery of life. They live in the spirit of the little girl who said:

> "I gave a little party this afternoon at three;
> Twas very small, three guests in all, just I,
> myself and me.
> Myself ate up all the sandwiches, while I
> drank up the tea,
> And it was I who ate the pie, and passed
> the cake to me."

My goal every day is to unlock myself and to unravel the mystery of life's treasures. We often come to the fork of life's road and cannot decide which way to turn. There are decisions to be made and sometimes hard to decide. We make choices which allow us to get lost. To me the key is finding things to unlock myself. Every day I come home to unlock myself again. I have several "keys" that open the mysteries of life to me in marvelous ways.

Key #1- Pet Love It is my wife's and my contention that if everyone had a dog or cat they would be okay. They would receive the total affirmation they need. Animals communicate with us in a language of the heart. How great it is to be welcomed home by a pet: the dog that is so vigorously wagging his tail that his whole body wiggles or the cat that is so determined to be recognized that she continues to meow until she receives a hello. We've always been a two dog family.

As we reach down to our pets, we are uplifted in mind and heart. Petting dogs and cats calms them and also reduces our stress, a reduction which is often reflected in lower blood pressure and peaceful feelings.

Key #2 – Nature and Relaxation. Recently, we added a therapeutic spa to our back yard. It totally unlocks me after a long day. It's also helped me to discover the power of star gazing. For a long time people have used stars to find their way at night. Many a lost soul has been guided by the North Star or the Big Dipper. If we watch the sky at night, we can see thousands of twinkling stars. They remind us how small we are. They remind us of the vastness of the universe, of the power and beauty that surround us.

Starlight in the sky, or reflected on a lake, can comfort us when we hurt and need unlocking. With sage and open arms, nature accepts our sorrow, no matter how we express it. Starlight, like all of nature, reflects a light that comes from way beyond us. It is that light that heals us in a deep and quiet way and unlocks the mystery.

Stay on the Road

Roads are among the most important assets of any nation. Choose a country without highways and you most likely will find people living in poverty in isolated towns and villages. Look at China, one of the oldest civilizations on earth, yet one of the least developed for many years. One main reason for China's backwardness is that they built walls instead of roads.

Let's compare a nation's roads to our personal infrastructure:

First, roads are necessary for the progress of a people. One of the primary reasons America developed so quickly from a wild frontier land to the strongest nation the world has ever known is the fact that we built highways and expressways up, down and across the country. The saying, "All roads lead to Rome," explains in large part the fact that Rome was a world power for so long. The history of Egypt would have been very different had the Egyptians built roads instead of pyramids.

Recently I heard a TV program which had been prepared by some of the leading scientists of our day. They traced the marvelous mechanical and scientific advancement of our generation and then concluded: "We have built a bright, shiny world OUTSIDE; but have failed to build ourselves INSIDE, and now our world is about to crush us to death."

Spirituality is the super highway to an individual's development. I know of some communities that let their churches close, only to discover that the later other worthwhile elements of the community also disappeared. We need to keep our personal road to spirituality open for our continued and complete development.

Second, roads bring us closer together. There was a time when we were widely separated even though we lived only 50 miles apart. Now we think nothing of driving that far to have dinner with friends. Roads make the difference.

One of the things I hate more than almost anything is prejudice. I have no respect for any person who thinks he is better than another person. Our nation has suffered at the hands of those who sow discord and division. I believe that there will come a time when racial strife, bitter conflicts between capital and labor, denominational narrowness, and all other things that separate us will disappear. The answer lies in drawing closer together and understanding one another. We might call that the road to acceptance.

Third, roads make traveling easier and pleasant. I often hear previous generations talk about how they used to have to push the car when they were stuck on some muddy dirt trail. Today roads are passable, and help is available everywhere when needed.

Over the years my work has centered on helping people who are stuck on the road of life. I have talked to people who believe they can break the moral laws and live a happy and free life. When they realize how wrong that theory is they then say that they want to get back "on the right path."

Any road is easily traveled in fair weather. But we get slowed down when the rains come. Sooner or later in life, sorrows, disappointments, and upsetting experiences may come. I have yet to see one person who could not go on if he or she were on "the right road"

Finally, roads carry us to new places. Roads get us "on the way." I can get on I-65 in Louisville and start traveling north and I can say that I am on the way to Indianapolis. That does not mean I have arrived at my destination. There may be many who are ahead of me on the expressway, but, though I am behind, I can still say I am "on the way." Roads take us places.

I might hit a pothole on life's road to greater harmony but if I get up and start again, I can still lay claim to being on the way. As long as I am moving in the right direction I insist that I am on the way. George Washington fought nine battles and lost six. But he won the war because he got up and kept fighting after each defeat.

It is very helpful for each of us to stop for a period of serious thinking about where we are going. There are a lot of people racing up blind alleys. And since life is a one-way street and no one can turn around and come back, those people end up in frustration and defeat. Not only does the right road lead us to a successful, free and happy life on this earth, it keeps us on the way to a life beyond.

A Well Balanced Life

There are four important facets to every well-balanced life: work, play, love and worship. We have just one life to live, and each day is a blessing. These facets practiced daily will sustain a well balanced life.

WORK - Uselessness is probably the most destructive state in which a person can exist. All of us have dreamed of the time when we could do as we please and not be compelled to work at anything. When such thoughts come into my mind, I remind myself of the story of the little boy who had been playing outside. He came into the house and was getting in his mother's way. She suggested to him that he go back out into the yard. He asked, "What can I do?" She replied, "Do whatever you want to do." He answered, "Mama, I am tired of doing what I want to do."

There is a lot of food for thought in that little story. We need obligations and responsibilities in life. We need burdens to bear, dreams to dream, and work to accomplish.

PLAY – But work alone is not sufficient. The second part of life which is vital is play. We are familiar with the old proverb: "All work and no play make Jack a dull boy." Play includes rest, relaxation, and a change of activity. Without play one becomes tense, stressed and fatigued. One-fourth of life should be given to play. We need to remember that the word "recreation" really means re-creation. We need to learn to release ourselves in some activity that we really enjoy. It is a pitiful person who has forgotten the meaning of fun and is unable to play.

Many people are familiar with the popular folksinger, Mac Davis. One of the songs that he made famous goes like this:

> You got to stop and smell the roses,
> You got to count your many blessings every day –
> You're gonna find the way to Heaven is
> A rough and rocky road
> If you don't stop and smell the roses along the way.

The problem is, we get so busy with the work of life that we forget about the flowers and the beauty of life. Sometimes in the work of making a living, we forget to make a life.

LOVE - Love is the third facet of a well balanced life. Ultimately, human survival on this earth depends upon genuine love. Love gives one the strength to cope with the hardships of human existence while hate defeats a person even before the struggle begins. Love gives life purpose for being here.

Don't ever forget to love yourself first. That means that you keep yourself worthy of your own self-respect. An old minister used to pray, "Oh Lord, give me a high opinion of myself."

In loving ourselves, we are not being selfish. The selfish person is only interested in him or herself and finds little pleasure in giving and great pleasure in taking. The selfish person looks at the world only from the standpoint of what he or she can get out of it, judging everything in terms of its usefulness to him or her. Selfishness is really the opposite of self-love. In fact, the selfish person is not even capable of loving himself much less anyone else. Selfishness leads one to become a nobody.

Self-love makes one know that he or she is somebody. You are a person in your own right. As you discover your own worth, you really begin to discover life. Self-love opens us up for relationships.

WORSHIP - Worship renews the spirit as sleep renews the body. Helen Hayes, the queen of the American theater, told of an experience that she had in a church when she was facing her greatest sorrow. Her daughter was ill and was slowly reaching the terminal stage. Only a mother could understand the ordeal that Helen Hayes was experiencing. She was driven to distraction with worry and went to a church to pray. She looked around and saw a number of people upon whose faces she witnessed trouble and sorrow. She realized that life had not been kind to many of them and that they were there in God's House seeking renewal. Then she wrote: "It seemed, as they prayed, that their worn faces lighted up and they became vessels of God. In my need, I gained strength from the knowledge that they too had needs and I experienced a flood of compassion for them."

Ms. Hayes beautifully summed up the meaning of worship in those words: "I gained strength. I experienced a flood of compassion." In time of great need, people do live through worship. Consecration, meditation, contemplation, adoration, intercession, supplication, thanksgiving, and silence – all of these are part of worship.

We receive from life, from every experience, from each interaction according to what we have given. When we commit ourselves fully to the four facets of work, play, love and worship, we will be blessed. When we give ourselves wholly to any moment, our awareness of reality will be heightened and our lives will find balance.

The Best is Yet to Be

One of the classic poems of all time is Robert Browning's "Rabbi Ben Ezra" in which he said:
"Grow old along with me!
The best is yet to be,
The last of life,
　　　　for which the first was made.
Our times are in his hand
Who saith: 'A whole I planned
Youth shows but half; trust God;
See all, nor be afraid!'"
We might think, "Of course, Robert Browning could write those words, he had his beloved Elizabeth." The truth is, when Browning wrote "Grow Old Along With Me," Elizabeth had been dead for three years. The great poet's life was shattered. During those three years he had accomplished very little. At the time he was well past the age of 50. He wanted to run away and hide, but he faced up to his own character defects and decided that he should be more a man than a coward. He began thinking of a man whom he had admired for many years, the twentieth-century scholar, Rabbi ben Ezra. Among other things Rabbi ben Ezra had preached, "Approach the twilight of life with joy and hope. Approach the last of life with eagerness, not gloom. For the last of life is the best of life. Trust God and be not afraid."

Browning was inspired to write a poem on those teachings and he gave himself completely to it. Many of us feel it became his crowning effort. The point is that he was alone when he wrote "Grow Old Along With Me" yet he filled the poem with hope for his future.

You can divide life into two major time frames. The years before 60 are the years of physical as well as mental vitality. The years after 60 are often years of less physical activity, slightly less mental acuity but greatly increased spiritual awareness.

Look at the age of 60, which I consider sort of the dividing line. For many it is really the time of new birth – the time to start new hobbies, develop new interests, and even begin new careers. For others, it will be the beginning of the "shriveling-up" era of their life. Disease becomes more prominent. Some people begin to think of themselves as being weaker and sicker. It can be a time of giving up instead of growing up.

Later we come to the time of retirement. We can think of ourselves as "rocking chair" cases. But remember Thomas Edison created the electric light bulb in his mid-sixties. This really is the time to think up new ideas – the time to re-tire. It is time to forget about that big rest and begin tuning in on the millions of ideas waiting to be discovered in this glorious universe.

The period after the age of 60 can be a time of mental and spiritual growth that we have never known before. Out of a wise intellect can come our greatest ideas, our deepest understandings, and our finest joys. These are the years that prove how you have lived and what you have packed into that life. Never believe that you just dry up and bend over at the age of 70. Above all things at this age get happiness. It is the most wonderful of all lifesavers.

> "Age is like a mountain high;
> Rare is the air and blue –
> A long, hard climb and a little fatigue –
> But, oh! What a wonderful view!"
> *-Author Unknown*

Whatever your age, your major emphasis should be to continually bolster self-confidence. All of my life I have been a student of Abraham Lincoln. I believe he is the greatest American who ever lived. If you really know Lincoln, you know that his greatest problem was that he had doubts about himself, doubts which lingered until his death. Self-confidence was very difficult for him to attain, but he won out over his doubts and they never defeated him. There are several steps to real self-confidence, no matter what you age is.

1. **Set a major goal for yourself in life.** Forget about the fact that you have achieved goals or that you have failed. Begin right now and select a new target. Start saying to yourself and keep on saying it until you really believe it. "What I have decided to do, I can do."

2. **Do not waste worry making decisions.** Even if you make a mistake, it can be corrected.

3. **Talk about your fears to somebody else.** The verbal expression of your fears often deflates them.

4. **Do not forget how to laugh.** Laugh both at yourself, with other people, and at your world and its futility.

5. **Remember that other people have the same doubts, worries and problems that you have.** Be sympathetic, kind and thoughtful of others. Not only should you think of what you can do for yourself and what you can accomplish, but also perform an act of kindness that will bring strength and courage to another life.

6. **Remember that you are never alone.** Even if your loved ones are too busy for you, or if you have only a few friends, there is a power and comfort to be found in frequent prayer and meditation.

Go back to Robert Browning's beautiful poem: "Grow old along with me! The best is yet to be." Let's emphasize the line, "The best is yet to be." No matter what your life is, believe that your present age is the best age. And it is very likely to be.

Gotta Have Hope

Hanging in the Tate Gallery in London is George Frederick Watts' great painting entitled, "Hope." It pictures a blindfolded woman sitting on the world, stricken and dejected. In her hand is a harp with all the strings broken except one. She is striking that one string and her head is bent toward it in closest attention to catch its sound. This is the artist's picture of hope, triumphant over the world's sin and sorrow, triumphant over anything and everything that can hurt a human being. When all else is gone, one still has hope left and hope can triumph.

There are many stories of people who were inspired by Watts' painting. One that I like tells of a man who had decided to commit suicide by drowning himself. On the way he saw this painting in a store window. He looked carefully at the blindfolded woman on her world of misery, playing the one string. He couldn't look away and gradually realized, "Well, I have one string – I have a little boy at home," and he turned back.

In one form or another, that story has been repeated countless times. No matter how bad life is, if we will only look, we can always find one bit of hope that is left and that hope can be the saving power in your life.

Life can weigh heavily on a person and can eventually break them down. Another painting is very inspiring is Jean Francois Millet's "Man with Hoe." Many believe the French artist intended to show the dignity of labor. Others see the painting as showing one who is weary, crushed and defeated. Look at the painting and you see a man leaning upon his hoe. That hoe appears to be the heaviest hoe one can imagine.

Add just one little letter of the alphabet to that phrase and instead of "Man with Hoe," you get "Man with Hope." We certainly would not eliminate hoes from the world. The hoe represents labor and labor is important. Sometimes we feel that life would be wonderful if we could give up our jobs and

Create a Better World

live in ease and comfort. It is not so. Someone has quoted Michelangelo, the great Italian sculptor, as saying, "It is only well with me when I have a chisel in my hand."

We are glad that we have hoes and that we have the opportunity to use our hoes. Unemployment is always a haunting horror. A painting of a person "without" a hoe would be worse – much worse. But along with our hoes, we also need a hope.

There is an old protest song, "Hang up the shovel and the hoe, Take down the fiddle and the bow." This is not the answer. Each of us needs our work. The hoe is not a hopeless instrument. It is quite the contrary. Those in the field with hoes are looking toward a harvest, a harvest that will feed and clothe them and their loved ones. Those with the hoe have a reward to look forward to. Hoe and hope go hand in hand. It is when we lose our hope that we lean on our hoes and gaze on the ground. Hoes are not made for leaning on. A hoe is for work and the hope for the harvest is what makes all the difference.

Andrew Carnegie was fond of saying, "Three generations from shirtsleeves to shirtsleeves." This means, the children of the wealthy have a hard time finding the moral equivalent of the struggles through which their fathers and mothers obtained their wealth. We are not born to be satisfied. When we are satisfied we become bored and boredom leads to self-destruction. We are made strong by the struggle. Look at the lives of the early pioneers who faced harsh climates, sparse land, and endless toil. Out of their efforts came a sturdy civilization. The unfriendly environment could not defeat them because in them was the hope of the civilization they were building.

Sir Thomas Buxton said a wonderful thing: "The longer I live the more deeply I am convinced that that which makes the difference between one man and another – between the weak and the powerful, the great and insignificant, is energy – invisible determinations – a purpose once formed and then

Create a Better World   121

death or victory. This quality will do anything that has to be done in the world; and no talents, no circumstances, no opportunities will make one a man without it."

Create a Better World

Think and Act Anew

New thought and new action – How simple it sounds and how difficult it is! Most of us tend to be shackled by old habits of thought, by the dogmas of the past. When crisis threatens, it is all too easy to go on acting or reacting as we did before.

Great rewards await men and women who can change the pattern of their thinking to meet new conditions and new challenges. I have proof of this in my own experience. When I first left my career in ministry as a Roman Catholic priest at the age of 41, I had no intention of becoming a fundraiser. I first became a hospice chaplain and thought I would remain in that ministry the rest of my days. I was asked to attend a fundraising school and later accepted the position of director of development of Hospice. Reviewing my life, I decided that I really wanted to make a difference by making things happen by helping the non-profit organizations raise money.

The decision to "act anew" was not easy. Some of my friends and family counseled against such a drastic step. I took it anyway. I have never regretted it for an instant.

Today, many of the people who come to me for help and advice are suffering from a kind of rigidity caused by blind adherence to old patterns of thinking and acting. They cannot adapt to changing conditions. They find it so difficult to bend that sometimes they break.

Quite often, in my efforts to help these people, I quote Abraham Lincoln's words, "We must think anew – and act anew." When problems beset us, or when there seems to be no solution, we must not react rigidly. We must not look at our difficulties from old, habit-worn, outmoded points of view. We must think anew, and with the new thoughts will come the power and confidence to act anew.

You may find much satisfaction in analyzing, planning and contemplation, but change only starts when you take the first step. Even a small step is important because small changes practiced consistently, transform good ideas into great results.

There is the story of an old man in a small frontier town who had lived in the same house for 50 years. One day he surprised everyone by moving into the house next door. Reporters from the local papers descended on him to ask him why he had moved. "I guess it was the gypsy in me," he replied with a self-satisfied smile.

A quote I read daily is wonderful:

> "Help me to fulfill my destiny
>   To the very best of my ability
> To live the rest of my life
>   With honesty, honor and integrity
> And to bring joy and happiness
>   Into every life I touch."

Be open to change, face your fears and give up controlling behavior. Focus on the success of others, be willing to keep learning, and be willing to persevere. Willingness creates honesty, self-awareness and open-mindedness.

Things That Matter Most

My mother recently had to move to a local nursing home as she copes with Alzheimer's disease. Life for her is a repetition of words and thoughts. Often when we visit with her, my siblings and I remind her and my father of the things they have given us that matter most.

We remind her of how she read to us. She read us the classics from Tom Sawyer, Huckleberry Finn, and Treasure Island to selections from The Book of Knowledge and The Bible. We remind her that she developed within us an appreciation for reading and education. This healthy addiction for learning has transformed our lives and kept life exciting as all of us are hungry to learn more every day.

We reminisce about how she gave us the gift of music. All three of us children received piano lessons and are proficient on the keyboard. We recall how Mom would make sure that we faithfully practiced every day as we developed a true appreciation of music.

We also tell her that if we had had all the material things that we wanted she would not have had a chance to do for us what she did, because she focused on the things that matter most. All of this showed me that today in our eagerness to give our children all the things that money can buy we are failing to give them the things that money cannot buy, the things that matter most.

This reminds me of a story that I heard some time ago. A woman was having a brunch for women from her church. She had a little girl six years old. When the women arrived, the mother put the little girl in her bedroom and told her to stay there. The little girl stayed but she got bored. After a long while she stuck her head out the door and said, "Mama, don't any of these ladies have a home?"

I find myself very thankful that my mother was a woman who had a home. She was there for us when we needed her.

We didn't have everything we wanted materially, but then, when you have a real home not much else is needed.

Emerson wrote a wonderful essay on "Gifts" in which he said, "Rings and other jewels are not gifts. They are apologies for gifts. The only gift is a portion of thyself."

What is the greatest thing a person can have? It is not money, because you cannot always hold on to it. It is not fame, because they will cheer you one day and sneer at you the next. But if you can have faith in yourself and peace in your heart, that is the thing that really matters when all else is gone.

A lot of people think if they can just get a new car or a new house or a large sum of money saved up, they would be happy. But, actually, what we really want is to be able to be deeply happy no matter where we live, what we drive, or how little we may have.

I was telling this to a man in my office and he said to me, "Where can one get that faith and peace that I seem to lack?" I told him that the place to get it is from those who have it. If you wanted to borrow some money, you would go to someone who has some money. The same is true of faith. Surround yourself with people who exhibit that faith and peace you want in your life.

When you spend time with people like my mother who are strong in faith and calm of soul you catch that, too. We gain strength from each other. And that is what matters the most.

Get the Most Out of Life

My goal is to live life fully and completely. The following ten principles have helped me get the most out of life.

1. **Be Responsible or Be a Victim**

   There are so many occasions when we would like to blame somebody (wife, children, parents, management) for our feelings. When we get frustrated, overworked, or angry, we want somebody else to take responsibility. This blaming and not taking responsibility keep us in the role of victim. When we accept the difficult message that our feelings are ours to deal with and no one else's, self-improvement begins.

2. **Remember the Power of Hope**

   We must admit life is often difficult and painful. But these facts do not describe all of life, and they do not determine how we respond to these trials. The sun rises warm and bright after a cold and dark night. The open, generous smile of a small child reaches into the soft part of us all. As Robert Frost said so well, "I always entertain great hopes."

3. **I Just Can't**

   A wise counselor once told me that whenever he knew he had to say no to a request he was unwilling to agree to, he used the very effective phrase, "I just can't," which people accepted. If they persisted, he would say again, "I just can't." No explanations were needed. Another friend uses a similar phrase when she has to say no to something. She simply says, "Don't go there." Realizing our limitations allows us to get more out of life.

4. **Take a Vacation Every Day**

   In Micronesian, there's a word, "kukaro," which has no corresponding word in English. When people say they are going to "kukaro," they mean they are going to relax, sit around, and hang out. They are being, not doing. What relaxing thing can you do today?

5. **Notice What Bugs You**

   We often get so stressed by the silliest things. We can eliminate a great deal of stress from our lives by simply knowing what bugs us. We then learn not to sweat the small stuff.

6. **Focus on Your Blessings**

   We are often so caught up in the pursuit of more -- more money, more toys, and more prestige -- that we forget about our many blessings. Think of the beauty of a sunrise or a sunset, or a walk by the river, or being with your best friend. What riches and blessings are with you this moment?

7. **Be Present**

   Pay close attention to each person and each activity that you encounter today. It's not what we do today, but how we do it that counts.

8. **Find a Way to Laugh Every Day**

   They say that people who laugh a lot live longer than do the sour-faced. When we laugh together, gratitude comes more easily, companionship thrives, and all praise is sincere. Laughter's joy celebrates the moment we are living right now.

9. **Keep Learning**

   Every day I ask myself what have I learned. My best habit is that I am an avid reader. My goal is to take the time to gather moments and opportunities I too often discard and waste and weave them into something beautiful.

10. Give

When we express love and kindness to others, we feel more love toward ourselves. We may not understand just how it works, but it does. Give to the world all you have, and the best will come back to you.

PRESENTATIONS AND PRODUCTS

♥ ♥

Bob Mueller's presentations are tailored to meet your organizations needs.   Topics include:

- Positive Living
- Stress Management
- Motivation
- Personal Growth
- Spirituality

To schedule a speaking engagement, please contact Bob at bobmueller@insightbb.com or write to:

Positively Speaking Enterprises
3902 Keal Run Way
Louisville, KY   40241-3031
Or call (502) 640-7810

Create a Better World

Books

Look Forward Hopefully - $14.95

Sensible, heartening and inspired advice on how to live more fully and calmly in the troubled world that is ours. Each of these reflections points out directions for those who are crowding life's road seeking light and truth. Topics include:
- Principles to Live By • Twelve Steps to Peace
- Enthusiasm Reaches Goals • Why We Worry

The Gentle Art of Caring - $14.95

Learn how to be a warmer, more lovable person, how to communicate better, how to get along with others. These clues for getting close apply to friend and friend, husband and wife, parent and child. In this book you will discover:
- Steps to Self Confidence
- What Gives You Strength
- A Maturity Check-Up
- The Mindsets We Live By
- How to Get What You Want

Book Order Form

Title	Qty
Look Forward Hopefully	_____
The Gentle Art of Caring	_____
Create a Better World	_____

Order Quantity		_____
	X	$ 14.95
Order Total		$ _____
Kentucky Residents add 6% sales tax		$ _____
Shipping & Handling - $2.00 per Book		$ _____
Total		$ _____

Please make check payable to PSE Publishing.

Mail Order Form to:

PSE Publishing
3902 Keal Run Way
Louisville, KY 40241-3031

Create a Better World